Social Issues
in Literature

Genocide in Elie
Wiesel's *Night*

Other Books in the Social Issues in Literature Series:

Social Issues in Literature

Genocide in Elie Wiesel's *Night*

Louise Hawker, Book Editor

GREENHAVEN PRESS
A part of Gale, Cengage Learning

GALE
CENGAGE Learning·

Detroit • New York • San Francisco • New Haven, Conn • Waterville, Maine • London

Christine Nasso, *Publisher*
Elizabeth Des Chenes, *Managing Editor*

© 2009 Greenhaven Press, a part of Gale, Cengage Learning

Gale and Greenhaven Press are registered trademarks used herein under license.

For more information, contact:
Greenhaven Press
27500 Drake Rd.
Farmington Hills, MI 48331-3535
Or you can visit our Internet site at gale.cengage.com

For product information and technology assistance, contact us at

Gale Customer Support, 1-800-877-4253
For permission to use material from this text or product, submit all requests online at
www.cengage.com/permissions

Further permissions questions can be emailed to permissionrequest@cengage.com

Articles in Greenhaven Press anthologies are often edited for length to meet page requirements. In addition, original titles of these works are changed to clearly present the main thesis and to explicitly indicate the author's opinion. Every effort is made to ensure that Greenhaven Press accurately reflects the original intent of the authors. Every effort has been made to trace the owners of copyrighted material.

Cover photograph © Matthew Mendelsohn/Corbis.

LIBRARY OF CONGRESS CATALOGING-IN-PUBLICATION DATA

Genocide in Elie Wiesel's Night / Louise Hawker, book editor.
    p. cm. -- (Social issues in literature)
    Includes bibliographical references and index.
    ISBN 978-0-7377-4394-4 (hardcover)
    ISBN 978-0-7377-4393-7 (pbk.)
    1. Wiesel, Elie, 1928- Nuit. 2. Genocide in literature. 3. Wiesel, Elie, 1928---Childhood and youth. 4. Jews--Romania--Sighet--Biography. 5. Holocaust, Jewish (1939-1945)--Romania--Sighet--Personal narratives. 6. Sighet (Romania)--Biography. I. Hawker, Louise.
    DS135.R73.W54634 2009
    940.53'18092--dc22
                                                          2009005240

Printed in the United States of America
    2 3 4 5 6   14 13 12 11 10

ED103

Contents

Chapter 1: Background on Elie Wiesel

Simon P. Sibelman

Elie Wiesel was a devout believer in the Jewish faith and
God, with a deeply rooted sense of spiritual identity instilled by the atmosphere in his family's home. His faith
in God was severely tested by his traumatic experiences
in concentration camps run by the Nazis. For ten years
he remained silent about what he had witnessed, until, at
the urging of a famous French writer, he wrote the memoir that eventually became known as *Night*. This book
was the catalyst for a lifelong career of writing and
speaking, bringing the Holocaust and other human rights
issues to the forefront of public consciousness.

Mark Chmiel

Wiesel's life can be distilled into three primary themes:
his youth in a traditional Judaic culture, his anguishing
experience in a Nazi concentration camp and his postwar
challenges as a survivor and refugee, and his commitment to sustaining testimony in a variety of genres.

Egil Aarvik

Wiesel's body of work stands as a reminder that the world
must remain vigilant and ready to counterattack future
attempts at horrific acts such as genocide. In 1986 the
Nobel Foundation honored him for his efforts to achieve
freedom and dignity for all who suffer.

Chapter 2: *Night* and Genocide

Chapter 3: Contemporary Perspectives on Genocide

Introduction

Were it not for a chance meeting between Eliezer Wiesel and French author François Mauriac, the groundbreaking memoir *Night* might never have been written. In 1954 Wiesel was working in France as a journalist for an Israeli newspaper. Mauriac was acting as an intermediary for an interview Wiesel was to conduct with the French prime minister. Upon learning that Wiesel was a concentration camp survivor and had already written an account of his experiences in Yiddish, Mauriac urged him to break his vow of silence and rewrite the book in French. Mauriac, a winner of the Nobel Prize in Literature and a celebrated writer in his own right, wrote the preface to the book retitled as *Night*. He, as well as Wiesel's agent in the United States, also promoted the book to numerous major publishers.

Their efforts were met with little initial success. The Holocaust was not a comfortable or welcome subject in the immediate aftermath of World War II. Further, Jews had cause for anger, given the lack of responsiveness by European Christians to stories of atrocities during the war. In an age prior to the Internet and immediate access to world news and events, it was easy for people to disbelieve, deny, or diminish reports of the death camps and the Nazi's program of Jewish annihilation. Once the camps were liberated, it was the liberating nations that had to deal with the reality of what they encountered.

In 1959 *Night* finally found a publisher. Although reviews were positive, the book still failed to find an audience. The trial of Nazi Adolf Eichmann in 1961 brought the Holocaust to the forefront of public discussion. During the next decade, Holocaust studies were incorporated in the curricula of many U.S. universities. *Night* became a mainstay of those studies. According to the *New York Times*, *Night* has sold 10 million copies since its introduction. Three million of those copies were sold since Oprah Winfrey selected *Night* for her book club in 2006. As for Wiesel's view, he believes *Night* reached critical mass in 1985 when he publicly admonished President Ronald Reagan for visiting Bitburg, a German military cemetery where members of the Nazi SS are buried.

Thus, with *Night*, began a lifetime of writing and service in the name of humanity, keeping the topic of genocide in the mainstream of public consciousness. Since 1960, Wiesel has become a prolific writer, turning out more than fifty titles, including stage dramas, novels, and essays. He has also developed an active career as a speaker, academic, and leading advocate for Holocaust victims and those who are targets of current-day genocides.

However, Wiesel is not without his detractors. The prose of *Night* itself has been characterized, as stated by literary critic A. Alvarez, as "a failure as a work of art," even while praising its documentation of human depravity and suffering. Ironically, it is the same simple and direct style of *Night* that has garnered acclaim for its power and depth.

Revisions to subsequent releases of *Night* have been met with criticism from some quarters. These critics cite changes that they believe sanitize some of the book's accounts, as a way of making the story more appealing to non-Jewish readers.

Still others have criticized Wiesel for appointing himself as the spokesman for Holocaust witnessing. And by continually revisiting the Holocaust, some say, Wiesel has not allowed the Jewish community to heal its wounds. He has also been judged for what some perceive as creating a career and an industry for himself from the suffering brought about by the Holocaust. On balance, Elie Wiesel can hardly be accused of building a lavish or self-indulgent lifestyle as a result of his writing and advocacy. The very act of publishing *Night* gave license to other Holocaust survivors to break their silence and come forward with their stories.

Wiesel has been universally acknowledged as a humanitarian dedicated to shedding light on inhumane treatment of populations wherever they occur. For example, at an April 2006 rally for Darfur, Wiesel said, "We, the Survivors of the Holocaust, know the consequences of silence, and this time we must all speak up for those suffering in Darfur." Wiesel's 1986 Nobel Peace Prize symbolizes the gratitude of the international community for his unceasing focus on human suffering and genocide. Wiesel has received numerous other awards and recognitions, including the French Legion of Honor.

Today, Elie Wiesel continues to speak out about world hunger, genocide, and racism. Addressing an auditorium full of students at Illinois State University in October 2008, Wiesel said, "These are all things that keep me busy as someone who tries to do whatever he can so that the world can save itself from all kinds of temptations. As long as someone is not free, my freedom is at jeopardy."

Chronology

1928

Eliezer Wiesel is born to Sarah and Shlomo Wiesel in Sighet, Transylvania, Romania. He is the third of four children and the only son.

1941

Wiesel begins his studies of kabbalah.

1944

The Wiesel family is deported to the Auschwitz concentration camp.

1945

Wiesel is transferred to the Buchenwald concentration camp. Months later, U.S. troops liberate him and other Buchenwald prisoners. Wiesel spends several years in a French orphanage.

1948

Wiesel begins studies at the Sorbonne in Paris and becomes interested in journalism.

1949

Wiesel visits Jerusalem for the first time.

1952

After his Sorbonne studies, Wiesel begins traveling around the world as a reporter for a Tel Aviv newspaper.

1954

During a meeting with the famous French writer François Mauriac, Wiesel is persuaded to break his vow of silence and write about his experiences in the death camps.

1955

And the World Stayed Silent is published in Buenos Aires, Argentina, in Yiddish.

1956

Wiesel is struck by a taxi in New York City and spends a year in a wheelchair.

1958

La Nuit is published.

1960

Night, the English translation of *La Nuit*, is published.

1961

Dawn, Wiesel's second book, is published.

1962

Wiesel visits his childhood home in Sighet. *The Accident* is published.

1963

Wiesel becomes an American citizen.

1964

The Town Beyond the Wall is published.

1966

The Gates of the Forest and *The Jews of Silence* are published.

1968

Legends of Our Time is published. Wiesel is awarded the Prix Médicis in France.

1969

Wiesel weds Marion Rose. Two of his sisters, Bea and Hilda, attend the wedding in the Old City of Jerusalem.

1970

A Beggar in Jerusalem and *One Generation After* are published.

1972

Wiesel's son, Shlomo Elisha, is born. Wiesel begins a four-year stint as Distinguished Professor of Judaic Studies at the City University of New York.

1973

The Oath is published.

1974

Wiesel writes a play, *Zalmen; or, The Madness of God.*

1975

Wiesel receives the Jewish Heritage Award from Haifa University and the Holocaust Memorial Award from the New York Society of Clinical Psychologists.

1976

Wiesel becomes the Andrew W. Mellon Professor in the Humanities at Boston University, a position he still holds.

1978

President Jimmy Carter appoints Wiesel as chairman of the President's Commission on the Holocaust.

1980

Wiesel receives the Prix Livre Inter from France. He also receives the S.Y. Agnon Medal and the Jabotinsky Medal from Israel.

1981

The Testament is published.

1982

Wiesel is the first Henry Luce Visiting Scholar in Humanities and Social Thought at Yale University, a position he holds for two years.

1985

President Ronald Reagan presents the U.S. Congressional Gold Medal of Achievement to Wiesel.

1986

Wiesel wins the Nobel Peace Prize. He and his wife Marion establish the Elie Wiesel Foundation for Humanity.

1987

Wiesel testifies at the trial of Klaus Barbie, a Nazi SS leader and war criminal who was known as the Butcher of Lyon.

1988

Twilight is published.

1990

From the Kingdom of Memory is published.

1991

Sages and Dreamers: Biblical, Talmudic, and Hasidic Portraits and Legends is published.

1992

President George H.W. Bush awards Wiesel the Presidential Medal of Freedom. *The Forgotten* is published.

1993

Wiesel delivers the dedication speech at the opening of the U.S. Holocaust Memorial Museum.

1995

All Rivers Run to the Sea, the first of two volumes of Wiesel's memoir, is published.

1999

And the Sea Is Never Full, the second volume of Wiesel's memoir, and *King Solomon and His Magic Ring*, a book for children, are published.

2001

Wiesel is awarded the rank of Grand-Croix in the French Legion of Honor.

2002

Wiesel inaugurates the Elie Wiesel Memorial House in his hometown of Sighet.

2004

Elie Wiesel receives the Commander's Cross from the Republic of Hungary and delivers the Final Report of the International Commission on the Holocaust in Romania.

2005

Wiesel receives the Man of the Year Award from the Tel Aviv Museum of Art and the Light of Truth Award from the International Campaign for Tibet. *The Time of the Uprooted* is published.

2006

Wiesel appears before the UN Security Council to call attention to the humanitarian crisis in Darfur.

2007

Wiesel is attacked in a San Francisco hotel by a Holocaust denier but is not hurt. The attacker is later convicted of a hate crime.

2008

Wiesel receives an honorary degree, doctor of letters, from the City University of New York and an honorary doctorate from the Weizmann Institute in Rehovot, Israel.

Social Issues in Literature

Background on Elie Wiesel

The Life of Elie Wiesel

Simon P. Sibelman

Simon P. Sibelman is associate professor of French and Holocaust studies in the department of foreign languages and literature at the University of Wisconsin-Oshkosh.

Elie Wiesel was born into a devout Jewish family in Romania. He became an avid scholar of kabbalah, a study that served to strengthen his sense of spiritual identity. When he and his family were deported from their home village of Sighet to the Auschwitz concentration camp, Wiesel began a long descent into questioning God and his faith. Ten years after his liberation from the Buchenwald concentration camp, Wiesel was urged by a well-known French writer to write about what he had witnessed. He broke his vow of silence and wrote his memoir, Night. *This is the first and most significant of the many books, speeches, and essays Wiesel would write.* Night *served as a springboard for Wiesel's career as a human rights advocate.*

Eliezer Wiesel was born to Shlomo and Sarah Feig Wiesel on 30 September 1928 in Sighet, Romania, a town situated in the Carpathian Mountains in northern Transylvania. The third of four children, Eliezer was the only male child. Two sisters, Hilda and Bea, had been born before him; his younger sister, Tzipora, was born when Wiesel was seven. . . .

Wiesel's parents represented somewhat dissimilar poles in the boy's life. His father was a shopkeeper and, despite adherence to traditional Judaism, Shlomo Wiesel's education had drawn him nearer to rational positions advocated by enlightened Jews. He urged his son to learn modern Hebrew and to become acquainted with the emerging canon of secular Hebrew literature. Wiesel's father was respected by the Christian community, who viewed him as a link to the town's Jewish leadership.

Sarah Wiesel came from a Hasidic family belonging to the Wishnitzer sect. Deeply religious, Wiesel's mother introduced her son to the Hasidic art of telling stories, but she had received a broader education. Though secular literature had been forbidden in her home, she developed a keen appreciation for the German classics and could quote lengthy sections from the writings of Johann Wolfgang von Goethe and Friedrich von Schiller. . . .

Wiesel's formal education began when he was three years old in traditional *kheder* (elementary religious school). Following his father's guidance, Wiesel studied secular subjects and also took violin lessons. At the age of twelve, he asked his father to find him a scholar who could initiate him into study of the cabala [or kabbalah], but he eventually found his own master in Moshe, the caretaker at a local synagogue, with whom he spent long hours in the evenings reading and discussing the *Zohar (The Book of Splendor)*.

Deportation: A Life-Changing Experience

In spring 1944 Wiesel and his family were deported from Sighet to Auschwitz-Birkenau [concentration camp]. Wiesel's descriptions of the traumatic end of Sighet's Jewish community capture not only his personal tragedy but the total destruction of Central and Eastern European Jewish life. In Auschwitz-Birkenau, Wiesel was separated from his mother and sisters. His mother and youngest sister were gassed on arrival, but the two elder girls survived the Holocaust and were reunited with their brother after liberation in France. Wiesel remained close to his father throughout their incarceration in Auschwitz, on the death march into Germany, and in Buchenwald [concentration camp], where his father died several days before the liberation of the camp on 11 April 1945.

Holocaust survivor and author Elie Wiesel, fourth from the front of the left column, walking out of the Buchenwald Concentration Camp in Germany, 1945. Wiesel was among a group of children and others liberated by the United States Third Army during World War II. AP Images.

Wiesel was evacuated with other child survivors from Germany by the American military, but their train was diverted to France on orders from Charles de Gaulle. Wiesel was sent to Ecouis in Normandy, where the *OEuvre de Secours aux Enfants* (Society for Assistance to Children) had established a home for Jewish child survivors. Then, in Paris, he found his eldest sister, Hilda.

Later Wiesel went to Taverny, Embloy, and Versailles, where he continued his studies and learned French. Introduced to François Wahl, then a graduate student in philosophy at the Sorbonne, Wiesel found a tutor in French literature and in philosophy. Moving to Paris, Wiesel was enrolled at the Sorbonne from 1947 to 1950, studying psychology, literature, and philosophy. He engaged in research for a thesis in comparative asceticism and traveled to India to gather material on the significance of suffering within the Hindu tradition. However, he never submitted the thesis.

Building a Postwar Career

While a student, Wiesel worked as a private tutor of Yiddish, Hebrew, and the Bible in order to support himself. Beginning in 1947, he also undertook work as a journalist, initially writing for *Zion in Kamf*, a Zionist newspaper in Yiddish. In 1948 he became an occasional correspondent for the French Jewish journal *L'Arche* and for the Israeli newspaper *Yedi'ot Akharonot*. In 1949 he traveled to Israel to cover the War of Independence, and in 1952 he reported on meetings between West German and Israeli representatives concerning war reparations. His experience as a journalist provided Wiesel with the rigorous discipline he employed in his subsequent writing. . . .

The Catalyst for *Night*

In 1954 an assignment for *Yedi'ot Akharonot* to interview French prime minister Pierre Mendès-France brought Wiesel into contact with an intermediary, the well-known French writer François Mauriac. That meeting set Wiesel on his life-long career as Holocaust witness, writer, lecturer, and educator. When he was liberated from Buchenwald, Wiesel had vowed to remain silent about what he had witnessed, and he kept that silence for ten years. His meeting with Mauriac proved the catalyst that released his memories and liberated his voice.

Over the next year, Wiesel wrote an 800-page Yiddish memoir, *Un di velt hot geshvign* (And the World Kept Silent), which was published in 1956 by the Central Union of Polish Jews in Argentina in Buenos Aires. On Mauriac's counsel, Wiesel revised and then translated the Yiddish text into French, giving it the title *La Nuit* (1958; translated as *Night*, 1960). . . .

Emerging Role as a Human Rights Advocate

In the 1960s Wiesel became increasingly recognized as one of the most significant witnesses to the Holocaust, his international prominence assured by prestigious prizes and awards. In France he won the Prix Rivarol (1963) for his novel *La Ville de la chance* and the Prix Médicis in 1968 for *Le Mendiant de Jérusalem,* while in the United States in 1965 he was awarded the National Jewish Book Council Literary Award, and in 1966 B'nai B'rith presented him its first annual Jewish Heritage Award for Excellence in Literature. In 1967 he was granted an honorary doctorate by the Jewish Theological Seminary of America, the first of many such honors.

His emerging role as a witness also drew him to assume a more active role against injustices and tyrannies. In 1965 he traveled to the Soviet Union in order to spend the Jewish High Holy Days with Soviet Jews. His experiences in Moscow convinced him that a climate of fear existed and that Soviet Jews lived with the threat of persecution or imprisonment if they openly displayed their Jewishness. Wiesel exposed their plight in a series of articles written in Hebrew for *Yedi'ot Akharonot,* subsequently translated into French as *Les Juifs du silence* (1966; translated as *The Jews of Silence: A Personal Report on Soviet Jewry,* 1966). The plight of Soviet Jewry became one of Wiesel's major concerns. . . .

In spring 1969 Wiesel married Marion Rose in Jerusalem. Born in Vienna, she was also a Holocaust survivor, and she served as the principal translator of Wiesel's French texts. In 1972 their only child, Shlomo Elisha, was born (Marion Wiesel had one child, Jennifer, from a previous marriage). As Alan Berger notes in *Crisis and Covenant: The Holocaust in American Jewish Fiction* (1985), fatherhood also brought Wiesel to explore the world of child survivors and the children of survivors in his novels. In 1972 Wiesel was awarded the Eleanor

Roosevelt Memorial Award and the American Jewish Committee's American Liberties Medallion. . . .

In recognition of Wiesel's contribution as a witness to the Holocaust and his unceasing efforts on behalf of assorted ethnic groups facing terror or murder, President Jimmy Carter invited Wiesel to become chairman of the President's Commission on the Holocaust in November 1978. That commission was succeeded in 1980 by the United States Holocaust Memorial Council, which became the inspiring force behind the creation of the United States Holocaust Memorial Museum in Washington, D.C. Under Wiesel's guidance, the commission also promoted the establishment of annual "Days of Remembrance" to recall and to honor the millions who lost their lives in the Holocaust. The first Day of Remembrance was observed in the U.S. Capitol Rotunda on 24 April 1979. Wiesel remained chairman of the council until he resigned in 1986. . . .

Recognized Internationally as a Humanitarian

During the 1980s Wiesel's essays and stories focused on moral and ethical issues. He frequently spoke out against the maltreatment of Soviet Jews, urging Soviet leaders to allow those Jews who wished to do so to emigrate. He highlighted the shameful existence of famine in a world of food surpluses. He spoke out against the suffering of African tribes, the injustice of the apartheid system in South Africa, the massacre and dispossession of the Miskito Indians of Nicaragua, the civil war in Lebanon, and the torture of children around the globe. He warned of the perils of nuclear weapons and the ultimate holocaust they could unleash. He protested the genocide in Cambodia and traveled to Aranyaprathet, Thailand, in 1980 in order to bring vital food and medical supplies to Cambodian refugees. He arranged a conference in Arizona in 1985 to explore the possibilities of providing political and humanitarian asylum to refugees fleeing brutal civil wars in El Salvador and Guatemala.

Wiesel's unceasing humanitarian activities in tandem with his vocation as witness to the Holocaust continued to win him national and international recognition. France honored him in 1983 by electing him a Commandeur de l'Ordre de la Légion d'honneur, and in 2001 he was awarded the Grande Croix de la Legion d'honneur, that nation's highest accolade. In 1985 President Ronald Reagan awarded Wiesel the United States Congressional Gold Medal, followed in 1986 with his receiving the Medal of Liberty for his significant contributions to American life. In 1986 the Nobel Committee conferred on him the Nobel Peace Prize.

Beginning in 1986, Wiesel was active with his wife in the Elie Wiesel Foundation for Humanity, aided by money from his Nobel Prize. This foundation funded a variety of international conferences and colloquiums that have dealt with the persistence of hatred, intolerance, and bigotry. In 1987 Wiesel traveled to Lyon, France, to testify in the trial of Nazi war criminal Klaus Barbie. In July 1992 he led a delegation to Belgrade, the Serbian capital, in order to investigate conditions in prison camps for Bosnians, and afterward he attacked Slobodan Milosevic's racist policy of "ethnic cleansing." In June 1995 Wiesel organized a conference in Venice, Italy, for thirty adolescents from regions of the world in conflict, dedicated to "The Leaders of Tomorrow." In December 1995 he organized a conference, "The Future of Hope," in Hiroshima, Japan.

Wiesel Focus of Criticism

Wiesel's constant efforts to address the suffering of ethnic minorities and other groups and to maintain a sharp focus on his role as witness to the genocide of the Jews have not always made Wiesel impervious to criticism and attack. Beginning in the early 1980s, Wiesel was accused by some critics and scholars of lacking acumen as a writer. A series of acrimonious confrontations erupted. Shortly after Wiesel and François Mitterand wrote *Mémoire a deux voix* (1995; translated as *Memoir in Two Voices*, 1996), the two became estranged because of Wiesel's disagreements with the French president's opinions concerning France's behavior in World War II; this rift was never fully healed. Kali Tal in her *Worlds of Hurt: Reading the Literature of Trauma* (1996) questioned in the name of radical relativism Wiesel's definition of "survivor." The American scholar Norman Finkelstein attacked Wiesel in his polemical *The Holocaust Industry* (2000) for allegedly seeking personal enhancement and enrichment and having misappropriated the position of spokesperson for Holocaust survivors. . . .

Wiesel Asks Us to Remember the Holocaust

Since the 1960s, Elie Wiesel has sounded a clarion call to remember the traumatic events he witnessed during the Holocaust. In his 1986 Nobel Prize acceptance speech, he said: "How are we to reconcile our supreme duty toward memory with the need to forget that is essential to life? No generation has had to confront this paradox with such urgency." Variously labeled the poet of the Holocaust, the voice of contemporary Jewry, and an eloquent spokesman for humanity, Wiesel has been called a modern prophet, who urges people to probe deeply into the individual and communal consciousness in an effort to redefine the human condition and to seek ways of making the human experience more godly. Wiesel's work has enriched the genre of the Holocaust novel by interjecting a mixture of narrative techniques—most notably approaches employed by French *nouveaux romanciers* (New Novelists)—that resonate with the Hasidic sensibility of storytelling. Philosophical and psychological issues pervade each tale, hauntingly echoing from text to text. Wiesel's novels highlight the profound moral responsibility survivors sense to preserve and transmit memory and suggest the burden of memory and the pain that can be passed to the next generation. They also work toward reestablishing dialogue between human beings, and between humanity and the Creator. Weisel's perspective as a survivor has intensified his view of humankind as never having fully emerged from the shadow of the Holocaust, and his huge literary output emphasizes that if the horrors of the past are not remembered, humanity's common future is forfeit.

Three Primary Themes Characterize Wiesel's Life

Mark Chmiel

Mark Chmiel is Adjunct Professor of Theological Studies at Saint Louis University and Adjunct Professor of Religious Studies at Webster University.

Elie Wiesel's life, asserts Mark Chmiel, can be divided into three primary phases: mysticism, trauma, and testimony. Wiesel's early years were spent immersed in the traditional Judaic traditions. As a young man, he experienced the horrors and deprivation of the Nazi death camps and post-Holocaust adjustments as a survivor and refocused religious scholar. These first two phases informed his third and current phase of witnessing and testifying against human suffering and violence around the world. Chmiel notes that the Holocaust has remained a prominent concern in American life largely due to Wiesel's efforts.

Three main themes of Wiesel's life [are]: his childhood in a traditional Judaic culture in Eastern Europe; his traumatic experience in a Nazi death camp and his postwar trials as a survivor and refugee; and his commitment to testimony in a variety of genres.

The Judaic Community

In their study of American character *Habits of the Heart*, sociologist Robert Bellah and his colleagues emphasize the importance of religion and other communities of memory in fostering bonds that might resist the peculiar individualism of American culture. Sociologist Edward Shils argues more gen-

Mark Chmiel, *Elie Wiesel and the Politics of Moral Leadership*, Philadelphia: Temple University Press, 2001. Copyright © 2001 by Temple University. All rights reserved. Reproduced by permission.

erally for people in contemporary society to nurture a greater sense of tradition, which has been undermined both by modern individualism and nationalism. Shils advocates a healthy respect for "substantive traditionality," which he describes as "the appreciation of the accomplishments and wisdom of the past and of the institutions impregnated with tradition, as well as the desirability of regarding patterns from the past as valid guides." Elie Wiesel's life and work have been rooted profoundly in such a substantive traditionality, namely, the Judaic community of memory. . . .

Because his father was a distant, though respected, figure, Wiesel felt closest to his mother, whom he considered "my sole ally and support. She alone understood me." Along with his three sisters, Wiesel lived in the polylingual world of Romanian, Hungarian, Hebrew, and, for daily intercourse, Yiddish. Years later, Wiesel testified to his abiding affection for his mother tongue: "I love speaking that language. There are songs that can be sung only in Yiddish, prayers that only Jewish grandmothers can murmur at dusk, stories whose charm and secret, sadness and nostalgia, can be conveyed in Yiddish alone."

In Sighet Wiesel grew up steeped in the Jewish religious tradition. He and his friends arose early in the morning to study the Bible and Talmud. Memorization of texts was privileged in a routine of study that went on for many hours each day. His sensibility was profoundly shaped also by the Hasidic mystical tradition inaugurated by Israel Ba'al Shem Tov in the eighteenth century. . . .

Wiesel also experimented audaciously with the secrets of the Jewish mystical tradition of the Kabbalah. Along with his young friends, he experienced an intense mystical yearning for salvation. They met frequently with their master, engaged in spirited incantations, and subjected themselves to ascetic practices, such as fasting, rolling around in the snow, and maintaining strict silence. Wiesel must have appropriated his mother's love for the Messiah, as he himself recollects, "I was convinced that every Jewish child must either bring the Messiah or become the Messiah." He was far more attracted to sacred writings than secular subjects in school such that his future path seemed clear: He would become a teacher in a yeshiva, with the modest hope of writing a commentary on one of the traditional texts. With his enthusiasm for mysticism, Wiesel paid little attention to the political events that were then engulfing Europe: "Tragedy loomed, but life went on. I paid little attention to the outside world. I was growing up, maturing, learning more difficult and obscure texts. [German leader Adolf] Hitler's howling failed to penetrate my consciousness."

Whereas other Jewish youth of his time were preoccupied with the secular variations of messianism in Zionism and Communism, Wiesel's own adolescent convictions were traditional and mystical, and these continued to influence his own interpretations of contemporary social and political events. . . .

Concentration Camps and the Postwar Era

Wiesel had been well acquainted with anti-Semitism in his hometown. Churches filled him with apprehension, and he knew that beatings of Jews were likely at Christmas and Easter. And even though Wiesel's mother maintained her fervent hope in the protective powers of the Messiah, Sighet's citizens witnessed omens of terror. As early as 1942, Wiesel's teacher, Moshe, had been deported from Sighet; he had survived a mass killing of Jews and returned to warn his people of the Nazis' murderous plans. Moshe's agitated testimony largely was ignored or dismissed by the town's Jewish population. Sighet's Jews could not believe that Hitler could eliminate Jews throughout Europe and so turned their attention to other matters, such as the hopes of diplomacy or Zionism. By the spring of 1944, the Nazis began their plan to exterminate the large Jewish population of Hungary. Jews were stripped of all their rights, forced into a ghetto, and then deported to Poland. It was in the Sighet ghetto, Wiesel later marvels, that he "truly began to love the Jews of my town. Throughout the ordeal they maintained their dignity as human beings and as Jews. Imprisoned, reduced to subhuman status, they showed themselves still capable of spiritual greatness."

Wiesel and his family endured the long railroad journey to a place of which they had never heard, Auschwitz [concentration camp]. He and his father were immediately separated from his mother and three sisters. During his first night in the camp, Wiesel was shocked beyond belief to see how Jewish children were being thrown alive into burning pits. . . .

Wiesel worked as a slave laborer in the Auschwitz-Buna camp, often accompanied by his stoic father, whose presence was enough to keep Wiesel alive. They and the other prisoners suffered the endless affliction of beatings, meager food rations, brutal humiliations, and the ever-present specter of death in the "selections" that led to the gas chambers and crematoria. When it was clear that the Russian Army would soon overtake Auschwitz in January 1945, the Nazis forced their captives to engage in a long march through the deadly winter cold toward German soil. Countless people died from starvation, exhaustion, and beatings along the march from Auschwitz to Buchenwald [concentration camp], including Wiesel's father. Buchenwald finally was liberated by American troops in April 1945, and Wiesel recovered in a hospital and faced dangers even there—the U.S. soldiers did not know that to give the emaciated survivors food with fat could prove deadly.

Wiesel presumed that no one in his family had survived and the thought of returning to Sighet was more than he could bear. Upon the invitation of French General Charles de Gaulle, Wiesel and others in a contingent of young Jewish survivors accepted an offer of resettlement in France. He soon learned that his two older sisters also survived. With home now being a French orphanage, Wiesel began his life over by resuming his religious studies:

> I rededicated myself to the study of the sacred works. Spontaneously, without thinking about it, I recovered my religious fervor, perhaps as a way of closing the parentheses on my recent past. Most of all, I needed to find my way again, guided by one certainty: However much the world had changed, the Talmudic universe was still the same. No enemy could silence the disputes between Shammai and Hillel, Abbaye and Rava.

He also continued his mystical quests with the itinerant genius Shushani, who was said to know thirty languages and who also taught the philosopher Emmanuel Levinas. Wiesel and his brilliant, inscrutable teacher might have spent weeks studying one page of Talmud, and it was from these exhilarating encounters in France that Wiesel admitted, "It is to him I owe my constant drive to question, my pursuit of the mystery that lies within knowledge and of a darkness hidden within light." During these first years in France, he worked as a Hebrew teacher and choirmaster. In addition to maintaining this continuity with his past, Wiesel made a necessary linguistic and cultural break: He began to learn French. For Wiesel, the French language "meant a new home. The language became a haven, a new beginning, a new possibility, a new world. To start expressing myself in a new language was a defiance." He studied at the Sorbonne in the late forties [1940s] and discovered the postwar philosophies of Jean-Paul Sartre and Albert Camus, whose existentialist doctrines, such as humanity's inescapable decision to confer meaning in an absurd world, would later give Wiesel a resource for reckoning with the destruction of his family, hometown, and culture. . . .

With his fluency in modern Hebrew, Wiesel found employment as a Paris correspondent for an Israeli newspaper. This work afforded him many opportunities to travel, including assignments to South America, North Africa, and India. In

1954 Wiesel received an assignment to interview French Prime Minister Pierre Mendès-France. Wiesel hoped that he could gain access to the statesman through his associate, the famous novelist François Mauriac. During Wiesel's first meeting with Mauriac, the Catholic writer began to talk about his faith in Jesus. Soon, however, the normally soft-spoken Wiesel could not restrain himself. He challenged Mauriac's faith in that one Jew who had been murdered two thousand years ago and whose death still moved hundreds of millions of people world-wide, whereas, just ten years earlier, millions of Jews were murdered with scarcely a protest. Wiesel then left Mauriac, but the novelist pursued and implored Wiesel to come back and speak of his experiences. Wiesel confided that he had decided not to speak about his time in the camps until he had maintained a vow of silence for ten years after liberation; he wanted to be sure he was ready to do justice to the event. Mauriac countered, "I think that you are wrong. You are wrong not to speak.... Listen to the old man that I am: one must speak out."

However, ..., he had already written a Long manuscript in Yiddish on the events that marked the demise of his family and people. Before the encounter with Mauriac, Wiesel learned that this Yiddish work had been accepted for publication in Argentina, to be published in 1956 with the title *Un di velt hot geshvign (And the World Stayed Silent)*. Eventually, Wiesel pared down his Yiddish memoir and translated it into French. Mauriac became a major advocate for the young journalist by using his own publishing contracts and authorial prestige to see that Wiesel's memoir would be published in France. Wiesel expressed gratitude:

> I owe him a lot. He was the first person to read *Night* after I reworked it from the original Yiddish. He submitted it to his own publisher, promising to write a preface for the book, to speak of it in the press, and to support it with all the con-

Originally published by the New York Times *on May 6, 1945, with the caption "Crowded Bunks in the Prison Camp at Buchenwald," this photo was taken five days after the United States Third Army liberated the camp. Wiesel identified himself within this photo as the man second tier from bottom, seventh face from left by the post.* National Archives and Records Administration.

siderable means at his disposal. "No one's interested in the death camps anymore," he was told. "It won't sell."

Thus, the initially disconcerting encounter with the devout French Catholic was instrumental in securing a major literary consecration for Wiesel. His memoir was published as *La Nuit* in 1958 and subsequently translated into English as *Night*. Perhaps more than any other, this volume introduced U.S. readers to the shattering effect of the death camps on a young person, his family, and faith. . . .

A Commitment to Sustaining Testimony

Although Wiesel was enchanted with the new State of Israel, he did not emigrate there. Upon recovering from an accident, for which he was hospitalized in New York in 1956, he decided to begin the process of becoming a U.S. citizen. While living in New York as a UN correspondent for an Israeli paper, he also wrote for the Yiddish *Jewish Daily Forward*. In addition to this journalism, Wiesel wrote novels—*Dawn, The Accident, The Town Beyond the Wall, The Gates of the Forest*—that explored the painful realities confronting Jewish survivors of the Holocaust. In 1965 Wiesel visited the Soviet Union to witness and report on the plight of the harassed Russian Jews and he worked tirelessly to mobilize the American Jewish community to take up their cause. Beginning in 1966, he became a popular lecturer on the Hasidic movement (as well as the Bible, Talmud, and other Judaic themes) at the 92nd Street YMHA [Young Men's Hebrew Association] in New York. He eventually collected these lectures in a series of books that helped introduce this branch of Jewish mysticism to a wider American audience. Although Wiesel was not immersed in the steadfast orthodoxy of the Hasidic Jews in New York, he maintained a fervent connection to the Hasidic movement, largely based on his devotion to his grandfather and his upbringing in that tradition. He also began to meet weekly with the renowned scholar Saul Lieberman to study Talmud.

In the spring of 1967 the world Jewish community was shocked by Arab threats to wipe out the Israeli Jews. That this was the second time in a generation that Jews had received a promise of impending extermination jolted the American Jewish community into giving greater public support to Israel as well as confronting the calamity of the Holocaust. When the war [Six-Day War between Arabs and Israelis] broke out, Wiesel traveled to Israel fearful of witnessing the final chapter of Jewish history. Instead, he was mesmerized by the swift Israeli victory and the army's capture of the Old City of Jerusalem. Because of America's enthusiasm for Israel's military prowess and the non-Jewish public's nascent recognition of the centrality of the Holocaust and Israel to Jewish life, Wiesel became an increasingly sought after speaker on cultural, religious, historical, and contemporary issues. His 1968 novel *A Beggar in Jerusalem* won the prestigious Prix Médicis, and the English translation was the first of Wiesel's novels to be reviewed widely and favorably. In 1969 in Jerusalem he married Marion Rose, who became the translator of his works. In 1970 he published *One Generation After*, a collection of essays that articulated the Jewish survivor's burden of memory and the excruciating ordeal of choosing between silence—because that which was experienced in the death camps could not be expressed in speech—and testimony—at the risk of the message falling on deaf ears or being trivialized by sensation-seeking media.

In the 1970s Wiesel enthusiastically identified himself with Jewish causes, especially the plight of the Jewish refuseniks in the Soviet Union. In 1972 his son was born; he decided then to work more vigorously to build a world worthy for his son to inherit, particularly by calling attention to a variety of non-Jewish issues of human suffering, from state-sponsored violence to starvation. He also stopped journalistic work and embraced a new career as a professor. . . .

By 1978 Wiesel had become so recognized as a powerful speaker on Holocaust-related themes that President Jimmy Carter invited him to chair his Commission on the Holocaust. Wiesel's charge was to lead a group of religious and civic leaders to envision an appropriate way of commemorating the European Holocaust on the national mall in Washington, DC. In this way, Wiesel's own objective of Holocaust remembrance was given powerful backing by a directive from the Executive Office. In 1979 he was appointed chairman of the U.S. Holocaust Memorial Council and thereafter played a key role in helping to establish Holocaust Remembrance Days in Washington, DC, with these annual services attracting the participation of government leaders and officials. In subsequent years, he received one award after another: the Congressional

Gold Medal (1985), the Presidential Medal of Freedom (1986), and the Nobel Peace Prize (1986), all of which enhanced his fame in the United States and around the world. In these national and international distinctions, Wiesel was lauded for his pursuit of remembering the Holocaust and speaking out on behalf of contemporary victims. Such eminence gave Wiesel much greater access to media, heads of state, and the general public.

He put his Nobel Prize money to work in a Foundation for Humanity that supported various humanitarian projects. He also organized international conferences on the theme Anatomy of Hate, hoping to illumine this human penchant for domination. He marched with Polish Solidarity leader Lech Walesa; conferred with Czech President Václav Havel and Soviet President Mikhail Gorbachev; and advised U.S. President Bill Clinton. He traveled to scores of universities to receive honorary doctorates and found time to continue to write novels. Throughout this period, he addressed human rights issues from South Africa, Bosnia, Burma, and Tibet to Central America, Cambodia, and Vietnam. Acclaimed as a "messenger to all humanity" in [American theologian Robert] McAfee Brown's honorific phrase, Wiesel achieved an unusual kind of celebrity in American culture, that of iconic witness to a twentieth-century atrocity. In addition to counseling the cultural and political elite, Wiesel shared his message of morality and memory in the broader American popular culture by appearing on Oprah Winfrey's talk-show and excerpting his memoirs in the Sunday newspaper supplement *Parade Magazine*.

Wiesel Honored as a Witness for Truth and Justice

Egil Aarvik

Egil Aarvik, who died in 1990, was a member of the Norwegian Nobel Committee from 1975 to 1990. He served as committee chairman from 1982 to 1990. His career also included work as a journalist and politician.

Elie Wiesel has become one of the most important advocates of peace of our time, according to Egil Aarvik, chairman of the Norwegian Nobel Committee in 1986. The Nobel Foundation honored Wiesel for his work to achieve freedom and dignity for all who suffer, regardless of location. He was also recognized for taking responsibility to alert humankind to the need for eternal vigilance in the face of evil. In his presentation speech below, Aarvik states that Wiesel's ability to rise above the suffering of the concentration camps is testament to his victorious spirit and solidarity with the oppressed.

Your Majesty, Your Royal Highnesses, Your Excellencies, Ladies and Gentlemen,

It is today [1986] exactly 50 years since the Nobel Peace Prize was awarded to the German public figure and pacifist, Carl von Ossietzky. That particular award was one of the most controversial ever made. The newly established Nazi regime in Germany was violently critical of the Norwegian Nobel Committee, and German citizens were forbidden to accept Nobel prizes in the future.

This type of reaction was in a way so predictable that it can be ignored. What we ought to be more interested in, on the other hand, is the type of reaction which came from coun-

Egil Aarvik, "Presentation Speech," www.nobelprize.org, © The Nobel Foundation, 1986. Reproduced by permission.

tries other than Germany. Many were of course delighted, but there were also many commentators who were sceptical. Leading figures in politics and the press expressed the opinion that Ossietzky was too extreme in his warnings and revelations. Some believed him to be a communist. In any case, it was argued, the cause of peace was poorly served by a Peace Prize which seemed to be a direct provocation of the German government.

The existence of such reactions was obviously partly a result of judging the [German leader Adolf] Hitler regime by current political and moral criteria. Most people were, in contrast to Ossietzky, unable to recognise the deadly threat to democracy which was developing. When the threat was at last recognised people were more or less paralysed by the "Hitlerroar", and had few resources to fight it with, other than the almost desperate appeasement politics represented by [British prime minister Neville] Chamberlain. During Nazism's formative years the general attitude was one of unsuspicious ambivalence. Of course one disagreed with Hitler, but when is one not in disagreement with politicians? And of course one was aware of the terrible rumours about the brownshirts' atrocities, but wasn't it necessary to evaluate this against the background of the extraordinary situation in the country? At least there was now a strong and active government, and Hitler was of course a democratically elected leader. . . . Most people feared some sort of unavoidable catastrophe. But only a few suspected the extent of what was happening—and it is precisely because of this blindness that the catastrophe was allowed to happen. [Playwright Henrik] Ibsen's buttonmaker [character in the play *Peer Gynt*] was proved right once again: ". . .it's when insight is lacking that the fellow with the hoof takes his best prey".

Carl von Ossietzky had insight. He has the courage and ability to tell of what he saw, and therefore acted as an unafraid witness for truth and justice. All honour to the then

Nobel Committee for awarding him the Nobel Peace Prize. His testimony was, however, also his doom—Ossietzky did not survive his meeting with the terrible regime which had established itself in the heart of Europe.

Wiesel Brings Message of Atonement

Today, fifty years later, the Peace Prize is to be presented to one who survived. In 1945, on the ashes left behind after the sacrificial flames which annihilated six million Jews, sat the seventeen-year-old Elie Wiesel, an only son of Abraham, an Isaac who once again had escaped a sacrificial death on Mount Moriah at the last moment. He will receive the Nobel Peace Prize today because he, too, has become a witness for truth and justice. From the abyss of the death camps he has come as a messenger to mankind—not with a message of hate and revenge, but with one of brotherhood and atonement. He has become a powerful spokesman for the view of mankind and the unlimited humanity which is, at all times, the basis of a lasting peace. Elie Wiesel is not only the man who survived—he is also the spirit which has conquered. In him we see a man who has climbed from utter humiliation to become one of our most important spiritual leaders and guides.

The Nobel Committee believes it is vital that we have such guides in an age when terror, repression, and racial discrimination still exist in the world.

With today's presentation of the Peace Prize, a bridge is built between the German who gave his life in the fight against what he saw was going to happen and the Jew who has dedicated his life to fighting anything that could lead to a recurrence of that same tragedy. It is appropriate that there is a Nobel Peace Prize at both ends of that bridge.

Elie Wiesel was born on the 30th of September 1928 in the Romanian town of Sighet in the Carpathians. He and his three sisters grew up in a peaceful family which was strongly bound by Jewish traditions and the Jewish religion. Elie was fourteen years old when the deportation of Hungarian Jews began. Sighet was now occupied by Hungary, and the town's Jewish population was packed, in the usual humiliating way, into goods wagons and transported to Auschwitz [concentration camp]. There he saw his mother and youngest sister sent to the gas chambers. Later, his father died while being transported to Buchenwald [concentration camp].

Through his books Elie Wiesel has given us not only an eyewitness account of what happened, but also an analysis of the evil powers which lay behind the events. His main concern is the question of what measures we can take to prevent a recurrence of these events.

Wiesel Concerned with Preventing Another Genocide

The terrors he encountered in the death camps, which were slowly revealed to the rest of the world, were something which was qualitatively new in the history of mankind. The Holocaust was a war within a war, a world in itself, a kingdom of darkness where there existed an evil so monstrous that it shattered all political and moral codes. It represented a new dimension. According to its theoretical basis, which could only have been the product of sick minds, it was a capital offence to belong to a certain race! This was previously unimaginable, but now the unimaginable was happening.

It is true that previous regimes had used brutal punishment against real or imagined opponents, but behind such measures there was always an element of logical—though perverted—reasoning. The punishment was the result of some injury or offence, either actual or potential.

But for the Jews—and, to a certain extent, the Romanies— the situation was different. Among the relics of the Nazi regime have been found registration forms used when arresting Jews. The usual details were noted down: name, age, sex, religion, address, and, of course, reason for arrest. In the last case only one word was entered, the word *JEW*.

The enormity of what happened is thus not only the sheer number of the victims; it is not only the existence of factory-like slaughter houses. No, the enormity lies in the philosophy which made this "industry" possible! It is this that Elie Wiesel wants us to understand. His mission is not to gain the world's sympathy for the victims or the survivors. His aim is to awaken our conscience. Our indifference to evil makes us partners in the crime. That is the reason for his attack on indifference and his insistence on measures aimed at preventing a new holocaust. We know that the unimaginable has happened. What are we doing now to prevent it happening again? Do not forget, do not sink into a new blind indifference, but involve yourselves in truth and justice, in human dignity, freedom, and atonement. That is this Peace Prize laureate's message to us.

Elie Wiesel's sojourn in the death camps ended in Buchenwald in the spring of 1945, when the prisoners were liberated by American troops. Together with a group of other Jewish children he was sent to France. His stay in France was part convalescence, part study: he learnt French and studied at the Sorbonne before becoming a correspondent with a Tel Aviv newspaper. He travelled to the USA as a journalist, became a correspondent with a New York Jewish paper, and took American citizenship in 1963. In the meantime he had published a number of books, of which *Night* (1956) was the first. His writings, which have been translated into many languages, now include twenty-six full-length books, together with a large number of articles, essays, and lectures. He has been awarded a number of honours and prizes.

Elie Wiesel is an honorary professor at City College in New York and has, in addition, a professorship in humanities at Boston University. He is the leader of the American Holocaust Commission instigated by the President of the USA.

Rows of dead inmates lie in the concentration camp yard in Lager Nordhausen, Germany, 1945. Soldiers walk down the cleared pathways, and bombed buildings line the sides. Myers/Bettmann/Corbis.

Biographical details are perhaps unnecessary in Elie Wiesel's case—he is best presented through his own writings and through his actions in pursuit of his call.

Naturally enough, it was his own people's fate which formed the starting point for his involvement. During the years, however, his message has attained a universal character. Presented as it is in different variations and in different contexts, it stands now as communication from one human being to humankind. Its involvement is limitless, and encompasses all who suffer, wherever they might be. The fight for freedom and human dignity—whether in Latin America, Asia, Europe or South Africa—has become his life's purpose.

A Duty to Learn from Lessons of History

This involvement is based on a strong feeling of duty to the lessons which history teaches us. It has been said that peoples or cultures who forget their history are doomed to repeat it, and it is against the background of his own experiences that Elie Wiesel now warns us of this. We cannot allow ourselves to forget the fate of those who died. If we do forget, we commit them to death once again, and become responsible ourselves for making their lives—and their deaths—meaningless. This warning has also a future perspective: we must not allow the unsuspicious ambivalence to return and open the way for an atomic holocaust. We cannot allow ourselves to be deluded into believing that the unthinkable will not happen. For it has happened once before. History has warned us.

The duty and responsibility which Elie Wiesel preaches are not primarily concerned with the fear of the terrors of the past repeating themselves. It is much more an engagement directed at preventing the possible victory of evil forces in the future. The creative force in this process is not hate and revenge, but rather a longing for freedom, a love of life and a respect for human dignity. Or as Elie Wiesel has said himself: "I will conquer our murderers by attempting to reconstruct what they destroyed".

No, Elie Wiesel's standpoint is not characterised by a passive obsession with a tragic history; rather it is a reconstructed belief in God, humanity, and the future. And it is truly a belief which is both hard-won and tested.

Elie Wiesel sat thus in the ashes after Auschwitz. The storm and fire had terrorised his life. Everything was in ruins. His family was annihilated. Two of his sisters were alive, though he was not aware of this at the time. He was homeless and without a fatherland. Even his identity as a human being was undermined—he was now prisoner number A 7713, a sort of shipwrecked sailor on a burnt coast, without hope, without a future. Only the naked memories remained. And, like Job in the ashes, he sat there and questioned his God—cast his agonised "WHY?" towards heaven: Why did this have to happen? And why should I have survived? Dear God, why were six million of your own chosen people sent to their deaths? Where were you when they hanged twelve-year-olds in Auschwitz, or burned small children alive in Birkenau?

He was seventeen years old, and how could a life be lived after what had happened? The sorrow was so great, and the experience of life so bitter. Indeed, he was only seventeen, but was already the lonely prophet of the *Lamentations*: "Is it nothing to you, all ye that pass by? Behold, and see if there be any sorrow like unto my sorrow".

But he was alive. And in time it occurred to him that there could be a purpose behind it—that he was to be a witness, the one who would pass on the account of what had happened so that the dead would not have died in vain and so that the living could learn.

Telling the Story That Was Impossible to Tell

The problem was that the story was impossible to tell. No human being could accurately describe the terror which existed in the death camps. To tell could thus easily become a betrayal of the dead. But to remain silent would be an even greater betrayal.

He remained silent for ten years. Then his profession as a journalist brought him into contact with the French poet and Nobel prizewinner, François Mauriac. This meeting led him to break his silence—at first with *Night* and then in the course of very short time with *Dawn*, *The Accident*, *The Town Beyond the Wall*, *The Gates of the Forest*, the play *Zalmen*, *A Beggar in Jerusalem*, and his credo *Ani Maamin*—"I believe".

All Elie Wiesel's books and publications are concerned with the same theme—the Holocaust is present in them all. As he himself says: "You can get out of Auschwitz, but Auschwitz can never get out of you". But, even though the theme is always the same, and even though the same story is repeated time after time, there is always a new approach which opens up new perspectives. There is a remarkable development in Wiesel's authorship. We see a forward looking development in a human being who regains his upright position and his individual identity.

In the beginning everything is night and dark. On the last page of *Night* he stands in front of the mirror and sees a face which is like a bleached skull. Even in *Dawn* the day doesn't dawn—the whole book is a fight with the darkness of night. The problem is constantly the same painful question: "How can one live a meaningful life under the weight of such agonising memories?" Is the German philosopher correct in stating that memory is in the service of everlasting agony? Was there no way forward to day and to light?

The answer comes slowly. We meet the first intimation of dawn in *The Town Beyond the Wall* where two prisoners, one of whom is mad and the other dumb, manage to find a means by which they can communicate with one another. The dumb prisoner breaks his silence and the lunatic shows that he perhaps isn't so insane after all. They build a relationship which is a salvation for both of them. The same thought is developed in *The Gates of the Forest* and *A Beggar in Jerusalem*, and, as the books progress, the light becomes brighter. The man raises himself up. The spirit conquers. The answer to the riddle of the night is not hate based on what has happened, but a believing and hopeful rebirth into future events. This is what he calls *The Refound Song* which appears in his credo, his *Ani Maamin: I believe in God—in spite of God! I believe in Mankind—in spite of Mankind! I believe in the Future—in spite of the Past!*

Recognizing the Victory of the Human Spirit

And with this hard-won belief he stands forward today with his message to all people on this earth. This is a message which not only awakens our conscience, but also inspires a limitless solidarity where individuals find one another in the labor of building a "Town Beyond the Wall" for the future—beyond the wall of evil and dark memories.

It is on account of this inspiration that Elie Wiesel has so successfully reached out with his message. I doubt whether any other individual, through the use of such quiet speech, has achieved more or been more widely heard. The words are not big, and the voice which speaks them is low. It is a voice of peace we hear. But the power is intense. Truly, the little spark will not be put out, but will become a burning torch for our common belief in the future. Truly, prisoner number A 7713 has become a human being once again—a human being dedicated to humanity.

And, once again, we have met the young Jew at the ford Jabbok in the book of *Genesis*—he who in the darkness of night wrestled with God, he who refused to release his opponent before his opponent blessed him and who left that place at dawn marked for life on his hip. It was to this man that the promise of the future was made from on high: "Thy name shall be called . . . Israel: for as a prince hast thou power with God and with men, and hast prevailed".

It is in recognition of this particular human spirit's victory over the powers of death and degradation, and as a support to the rebellion of good against the evil in the world, that the Norwegian Nobel Committee today presents the Nobel Peace Prize to Elie Wiesel. We do this on behalf of millions—from all peoples and races. We do it in deep reverence for the memory of the dead, but also with the deep felt hope that the prize will be a small contribution which will forward the cause which is the greatest of all humanity's concerns—the cause of peace.

Jewish-Christian Dialogue Can Be Achieved Only When Certain Conditions Are Met

Jack Kolbert

Jack Kolbert was a professor of modern and classical languages. Kolbert, who died in 2005, met Elie Wiesel while at the University of New Mexico. As a result of that friendship, Kolbert wrote The Worlds of Elie Wiesel: An Overview of His Career and His Major Themes. *Kolbert authored ten books, as well as essays on French culture and related topics.*

Elie Wiesel lived a sheltered childhood in the Jewish sector of Sighet, apart from neighboring Gentiles. As Jack Kolbert notes in the following excerpt, the Holocaust forced Wiesel and his family into interaction with Gentiles, the Nazis. Kolbert further states that after the terror of the anti-Semitic hostility perpetrated by the Gentiles, Wiesel was still able to emerge from that horror committed to working for greater understanding between Jews and Christians. However, he first asks that each side gain knowledge about its own history and respect the right of the other religion to exist. Further, Christians, namely European Christians, must admit their culpability in turning a blind eye to the Nazis.

One of Wiesel's major objectives as a writer is to help create an environment of greater mutual respect and understanding between Jews and Christians. But he believes steadfastly that this environment will be possible only if Jews remain true to their own faith, and Christians to theirs. Only from positions of strength and self-confidence can both forge a healthy, ecumenical relationship. Addressing himself "to a

Christian in search of prayer," Wiesel writes that "We need to live together in the past [to share the memory of past horrors like the Inquisition, the Crusades, the Holocaust] so that there may be a future. From days of destruction, we would move forward to days of creation."

Young Eliezer Knew Little About Gentiles

The childhood universe of Elie Wiesel in Sighet was a thoroughly Jewish one. He grew up in the Jewish sector of the town. His family had almost no dealings with Gentiles. He attended a Jewish school, knew mainly Jewish people, and his parents traded mostly with Jewish clients. For him the only holidays observed were those of the Hebrew calendar. Consequently, as he admitted, he knew almost nothing of the values outside of his thoroughly Jewish world:

> As a child I felt no animosity and surely no hate toward our Christian neighbors. In truth, I was profoundly ignorant not only of things Christian but also of the non-Jewish world in general. I did not know that Christians and Moslems both saw their roots as the history of my people, that the Land of Israel was the spiritual cradle of nearly half the world, that the role Jews played in history and civilization was so out of proportion to their actual numbers. . . .

During his childhood in Sighet, it seems—from everything Wiesel writes about that period of his life—that the Jewish community lived in some isolation from the neighboring Gentile population. The Holocaust catapulted Wiesel and his family into the vortex of Gentile-Jewish relations. From this forced relationship Wiesel learned a cruel lesson: to wit, the Gentiles were the killers, and the Jews their victims. Having discovered the full fury of the anti-Semitic world, he witnessed in the deathcamps the unleashing of the most terrifying example of hostility ever manifested by non-Jewish people of the earth against the children of Abraham in an already long history of persecution and pain. What he saw in the camps made the savagery of the Crusaders and the Inquisition pale by comparison. That he emerged from the harsh world of the Nazis as a man determined to work for the betterment of interfaith amity instead of for vengeance is a most remarkable happening. In lieu of leaving from the camps imbued with a desire for vengeance, he found himself filled with anguish and with the desire to help put an end to anti-Jewish hatred. [Literary critic] Ted Estess notes that the future author of *Night* tried not so much to seek revenge against the Gentiles for their violent criminality against the Jews but rather to understand their motives and to analyze the causes of their anti-Semitism.

Wiesel Faults Christians of Europe for Indifference to Nazis

Wiesel lodges two fundamental complaints against the international Christian community. First, he blames the Christians of Europe for their indifference; after all, they did almost nothing to halt the Nazis in their murderous genocidal campaign. Second, he explains that in its relentless effort to convert Jews to Christianity, the Christian community implicitly suggested that the Jewish faith was inferior to Christianity. Otherwise, why try to convert? That the converters have never stopped trying to convert Jews to Christianity was for Wiesel totally unacceptable behavior. Such behavior can only lead to anti-Semitism. Wiesel points out that when Christians call upon Jews to abandon their faith, they are effectively demonstrating little respect for the values of Judaism.

Christians Must Stop Trying to Convert Jews

Wiesel maintains that interfaith harmony can be realized only after all religious groups accept the right of other religions to practice side by side, each one practicing in its own individual fashion. Addressing his fellow Jews he wrote, "If we could find Christians to listen to us—I mean *really* to listen to us—I still hope we have enough arguments, enough reasons, enough intelligence and sensitivity to convince them that they will never succeed in converting us. It's a lost cause. It's silly . . . And we still live in the same world, respecting one another. But I insist: respecting one another." On another occasion he further expounds on his opposition to religious proselytism: "We had enough problems with converts. We do not want converts, we do not want others to convert us, and we do not want to convert others. We want Christians to be good Christians, Buddhists to be good Buddhists, and Jews to be good Jews.". . .

On many occasions, [Wiesel] reminds his readers that one of the reasons that Jews have remained relatively small in numbers when compared to the huge populations of Christians and Moslems derives from Jewish rejection of the notion that Jews must promote their faith among non-Jews. With a certain degree of bitterness, Wiesel also attributes the small number of Jews to the fact that for two thousand years Christians have decimated their Jewish brothers through campaigns of killing or through aggressive campaigns to convert them to Christianity. In fact, Wiesel marvels that the Jewish people survived at all, considering the obstacles they have faced in the past. His message is succinct: enough is enough; proselytizing and persecutions have proven to be exercises in futility. It is time that Christians accept Jews, once and for all, but it is time also for Jews to recognize the worth of their Christian neighbors.

The authentic Jew must resist the temptation to incorporate into Jewish worship certain customs inherent to Christianity. Likewise the authentic Christian ought not to incorporate into Christianity the traits peculiar to the other religion, especially if these traits are alien to their own religion. . . .

Jews and Christians Must Learn from Mistakes of the Past

In his vigorous arguments for a much more meaningful harmony between Jews and Christians, Wiesel paradoxically maintains that this harmony cannot develop until both religious groups are willing to take cognizance of their past history and to formulate a strategy whereby the tragic mistakes of the past will not be able to be repeated. Before Jews and Christians can improve their conditions of future coexistence they must appreciate their sins of history. They must also accept the significant differences that will always inevitably divide them (e.g., the question of the Messiah, the role of Jesus as the son of God, the immaculate conception, dietary regulations, etc.). Once they accept these differences, they can begin to dialogue about how to diminish their mutual animosities and suspicions. Eventually they will understand that it is preferable to live alongside of each other than to engage in mutually destructive warfare. Once both sides learn to tolerate each other's dissimilarities they will be able to develop positive interrelationships based on mutual respect. Just as Wiesel calls upon Jews to agitate against injustices perpetrated against Christians, he expects the latter to become involved in defending Jews who happen to be treated unjustly. . . .

Although history has provided too many examples of Christian indifference and of Jewish aloneness, Wiesel remains optimistic that the Gentile world is ripe for reform and gives every indication that Jewish-Christian relations can really be altered for the better. In the post-Holocaust era, his efforts to combat Christian indifference have borne fruit. Today he is heartened to acknowledge that at long last Christians have begun to comprehend that indifference to the tribulations of one people eventually leads to the suffering of all people, including the Christian majority. No less a Christian leader than the late Joseph Cardinal Bernardin, Archbishop of Chicago, wrote that Wiesel's collaborative volume (with Albert H. Friedlander), *The Six Days of Destruction*, shows that "The Shoah, while it is a uniquely Jewish event, also belongs to the entire human family. If we Christians are true to ourselves, then we will acknowledge that the pain and horror of the Holocaust are also ours."

Nazis Were Christians and Killers

Throughout his literature, Wiesel contends that the Holocaust is both a Jewish tragedy and a Christian problem. The Jews were the victims, but for the most part it was the Christians (at least nominal Christians) who were the killers. Until the Christians accept this incontestable fact, Wiesel avers that true dialogue between Jews and Christians is virtually impossible. Shocking though this allegation may be for some Christians, Wiesel even charges that the Holocaust is the logical result of two thousand years of systematic and doctrinal anti-Semitism sponsored wittingly or unwittingly by the Christian churches themselves. After all, didn't Germany, the nation most responsible for the Holocaust, always regard itself, since the early Middle Ages, as a Christian nation? And wasn't Germany the birthplace of Lutheranism and the site where the Protestant Reformation was launched? Didn't most Germans observe Christian rites, either as Catholics or as Lutherans? Wiesel argues, rightly so, that German history was inextricably bound to that of European Christendom. He insists that when the German people subserviently followed the Nazi program to destroy the Jewish population of Europe, their national psyche had already been fashioned not only by German patriotic fervor but also by their Christian heritage. And what about the other national groups who gleefully aided and abetted the Germans in their war to exterminate the Jewish people—the Poles, Lithuanians, Latvians, Ukrainians, Estonians, Croatians, Austrians, and the others? All of these people were part of Europe's Christendom. And of course Wiesel marvels at the public silence of the Vatican during [German leader Adolf] Hitler's genocidal campaign. Few church leaders in Germany and elsewhere raised voices of outrage to decry the liquidation of the Jews, Gypsies, and other "undesirables." How does one explain the taciturnity or the acquiescence of the international Christian world? These troubling questions permeate Wiesel's publications. He knew that international pressure can often be an effective weapon against a nation's misbehavior. Wiesel notes the example of how the Soviet Union, then one of the world's two superpowers, eventually yielded to international pressure and began to permit Jewish emigration. Once Hitler had been convinced that the non-Jewish world would allow him to proceed with impunity, he realized that he had a carte blanche to do whatever he wished.

Christians Must Remain Vigilant Against Anti-Semitism

Profoundly disappointed that the ecclesiastic leaders of world Christendom had demonstrated such callous indifference at the specter of Jewish destruction, Wiesel knew that the indifference vis-à-vis the Jews displayed by Christians throughout past history could conceivably continue for years. With consistency he has maintained "that [the Nazi plan to eradicate the Jews] was inseparable from the past of Christian, civilized Europe . . . the history of Christianity . . . is full of anti-Semitism. More than that—there would have been no Auschwitz [concentration camp] if the way had not been prepared by Christian theology." In similar vein he declared that the German concentration camps were the "climax of ten centuries of Christian civilization, of irrational contempt and hatred." In the same passage he voiced his conviction that the greatest humanists of the Christian tradition—[Immanuel] Kant, [Johann Gottlieb] Fichte, [Johann Wolfgang von] Goethe, Voltaire—"are guilty because they aspired to prove that the hatred of the Jews and love of man could be reconciled." The respected Wiesel authority, [Irving] Abrahamson, concurs with Wiesel's arguments and writes that "Wiesel recognizes, as have many others, that the flames of terror that swept all across Europe were the culmination of two thousand years of Christian civilization. . . ." Pointedly insisting that the Holocaust must be recognized as a Christian problem, the author of *Night* reminds his Christian audience that "all the killers were Christian." To this non-Jewish world he poses the following disturbing rhetorical question and his reply to it:

> Now was it the Christianity in them that made them killers? I hope not. But the fact is that they did not become killers in a vacuum. They were the outgrowth, a result of the 1800 years of a certain civilization, of certain teaching, of a certain tradition—of hate—and they became the example, the living example of what happens to people when they learn to hate. And that's a Christian problem.

Wiesel proposes the interesting theory that as Christians were destroying Jews, they were at the same time destroying their own faith too since their religion, like Judaism, was based on belief in the sanctity of human life and on love for one's fellow men. In his usual lapidary [short, precise, and elegant] style, the writer summed up his accusation against the Christian world like this: "What mankind did not foresee was that when the world kills Jews, it kills itself."

Given all of the dismal facts handed down to us from history Wiesel believes that true dialogue between Jews and Christians will never take place until Christians accept some degree of responsibility for the Holocaust. He believes also that Christians will have to take concrete steps to suppress anti-Semitism to the extent that its roots can be found in certain Christian doctrines.

Social Issues
in Literature

CHAPTER 2

Night and Genocide

Night Is the Antithesis of the Traditional Coming-of-Age Story

David L. Vanderwerken

David L. Vanderwerken is a professor of twentieth-century American fiction at Texas Christian University.

In the following selection, David L. Vanderwerken states that the traditional coming-of-age story depicts a journey that leads a youth through life experiences, resulting in growth toward a positive and culturally idealized adulthood. The youth is armed with moral, emotional, intellectual, and spiritual knowledge that can be applied to assuming a position in a community. According to Vanderwerken, the concept of a coming-of-age story is turned inside out in Night. *While Wiesel begins life with a rich heritage and culture, it is quickly and violently taken from him. Instead of enriching experiences, guides, and mentors, Wiesel is plummeted into the depths of a world designed to isolate, depersonalize, and dissolve any sense of self.*

Traditionally, the story of maturation takes a youth through a series of educational experiences, some through books and classrooms, but most not, and exposes the youth to a series of possible mentors and guides who become, as [American author] Ralph Ellison puts it in *Invisible Man*, "trustee[s] of consciousness". Of course, Ellison's young man has trouble distinguishing the truth-telling mentors from the liars. Usually, however, such life teachers shape the youth toward a cultural ideal of adulthood. The function of education, [American author] Joseph Campbell tells us in *Myths to Live By*, is to

David L. Vanderwerken, "Wiesel's *Night* as Anti-Bildungsroman," *Modern Jewish Studies*, vol. 7, 1990, pp. 57–63. Copyright © 1990 by Joseph C. Landis. All rights reserved. Reproduced by permission of the publisher and the author.

shift the "response systems of adolescents from dependency to responsibility".... Often the initiation process is worked out on a journey, some movement through space, which has the effect of accelerating the rate of maturation, as in the case of ... [author Mark Twain's] Huck Finn. And often the journey implies a spiritual quest. The result is a story of moral, emotional, intellectual, and spiritual growth. Normally, the initiate not only achieves self-definition, but also social definition, ready to assume a role in a community, whether the youth is from the provinces, like Julian Sorel [in French author Stendhal's *The Red and the Black*], or remains in the provinces, like Sonny in [American author] Larry McMurtry's *The Last Picture Show*. In *Night*, Elie Wiesel inverts and reverses, even shatters, the elements of the traditional paradigm.

The very title itself implies a reversal since the *Bildungsroman* [coming-of-age story] usually opens out into day, illumination, awareness, life. Instead, *Night* leads us into darkness and death. While the traditional raw initiate grows out into a knowledge of the richness, fullness, complexity, and multivariety of life—its open-ended possibilities—*Night* starts out with a sense of richness in heritage and culture that is violently and quickly stripped away, denuded, impoverished. Instead of expanding and ripening, young Eliezer's life narrows, withers, contracts, reduces to enclosure. Instead of finding a self and a place in the world, Eliezer begins with a sense of self, located in a coherent, unified community, and ends up when Buchenwald [concentration camp] is liberated alone, isolated, and numb. Instead of becoming aware of his own potential, in touch with resources he was hitherto oblivious of in himself, Eliezer looks in the mirror on the last page and sees a corpse. The pious young boy of Sighet has been incinerated. And the corollary spiritual quest that usually leads to some satisfying accommodation or resolution ... leads in *Night* to the void. Instead of climbing the mountain, Eliezer spirals into hell. And at the bottom lurk only questions, no answers.

Jewish youth peer over a brick wall overlooking Mirowski Plac (Square) in Warsaw, Poland, October 15, 1941. USHMM Photo Archives.

Groomed for a Life of Study

The opening chapter introduces us to this pious and spiritual adolescent who lives in the eternal world, who knows more about what happened 5000 years ago than what is occurring in Hungary in 1943. The only son in a family of five, Eliezer has been groomed for a life of study, his future as a Talmudic scholar or rabbi tacitly understood. Now twelve, Eliezer feels impatient to delve into the mystical realm of Judaism, the Cabbala [or kabbalah], if he can find a teacher. Although his father refuses Eliezer's request to study Cabbala on the grounds of his youth, precocious or no, Eliezer finds a master in Moche the Beadle, the synagogue handyman. In Moche, Wiesel offers an apparently traditional mentor character, the sage who will guide the initiate through the gates of truth: "It was with him that my initiation began". Moche is a Socratic sort of teacher, asking challenging and paradoxical questions that have no easy answers, if any at all. He tells Eliezer that the answers to all our ultimate questions are within ourselves. As a result of their studies, Eliezer says, "a conviction grew in me that Moche the Beadle would draw me with him into eternity". Suddenly Moche vanishes, deported in a cattle car with other foreign Jews, presumably to a work camp.

Just as suddenly, months later, Moche reappears in Sighet having escaped from the Gestapo, and he no longer talks of "God or the Cabbala, but only of what he had seen". Wiesel now reveals Moche's significance as Eliezer's mentor, neither as tutor of the verities of the ancient sacred texts, nor as agent of Eliezer's developing self-knowledge, but as witness and prophet of the reality of the Holocaust, a reality Sighet is not only oblivious of, but also refuses to believe. Consciousness simply reneges at Moche's preposterous tales of mass murder. The town dismisses him as mad; in Wiesel's withering refrain, "life returned to normal". Although Eliezer continues to pursue the truth of the eternal as Moche-I had taught him, it is the truth of temporal fact taught by the Lazarus-like Moche-II—his insights into *l'universe concentrationnaire*, the kingdom of night—that will prove to be the most imperative, the most influential, perhaps the most authentic in Eliezer's near future.

That, for Wiesel, only the mad could imagine the mad truth finds reinforcement in the figure of Madame Schächter on the train to Auschwitz [concentration camp]. In chapter two, her hysterical shrieks of furnaces and flames are received like Moche's stories, an obvious consequence of madness. After all, she has been separated from her family. Finally, some of the people beat her into silence. Yet as the train nears its destination, she rouses to scream again, "Jews, look! Look through the window! Flames! Look!" Eliezer does look and realizes that Madame Schächter's cries all along have been premonitions, not psychotic hallucinations, for now he sees the chimneys of what he will learn are the crematoria. This woman of fifty becomes an indirect mentor who provides Eliezer with another insight into contemporary truth.

Contradictory Advice

Of the other adults that Eliezer encounters in the camps, two stand out in offering contradictory advice on how to survive in hell. The first, the prisoner in charge of Eliezer's block upon arrival, makes a speech to the new arrivals that echoes the sentiments of innumerable, traditional moral sages:

> Have faith in life. Above all else, have faith. Drive out despair, and you will keep death away from yourselves. Hell is not for eternity. And now, a prayer—or rather, a piece of advice: let there be comradeship among you. We are all brothers, and we are all suffering the same fate. The same smoke floats over all our heads. Help one another. It is the only way to survive.

Comforted by this plea for faith, community, interdependence, civilization, Eliezer thinks: "The first human words". Yet are they the "teachings of our sages"? For this condition? In Buchenwald two years later, after the death march evacuation of Buna, Eliezer hears another sort of advice from a block leader, at a time when Schlomo Wiesel is dying. This sage counsels Eliezer to look out for number one:

> Here, there are no fathers, no brothers, no friends. Everyone lives and dies for himself alone. I'll give you a sound piece of advice—don't give your ration of bread and soup to your old father. There's nothing you can do for him. And you're killing yourself. Instead, you ought to be having his ration.

Of course, this is practical wisdom as Eliezer knows, but "I dared not admit it". Yet this is the ethical dictum of hell, into which Eliezer has been fully initiated. No ties are sacred.

Night's most powerful dramatization of an inverted mentor-initiate relationship is that of father and son. Schlomo Wiesel, respected community leader upon whom others rely for guidance and strength, represents the patriarchal Jewish father, a *mensch*, or as [Canadian-American author Saul] Bellow's Moses Herzog [character in the novel *Herzog* puts it, "a father, a sacred being, a king". Normally, the father helps the son make the transition in adolescence from dependence to independence. In the kingdom of night, however, the roles completely reverse; the son becomes the parent. In the end, the man whom others looked to has "become like a child, weak, timid, vulnerable". This reversal of the normal order is prefigured at Birkenau [concentration camp] when the veteran prisoner urges father and son to declare their ages to be forty and eighteen, not their actual fifty and fourteen, the better to survive Dr. Mengele's selection. Indeed time itself does warp, becoming nightmare time, accelerating human changes. "How he had changed! His eyes had grown dim," comments Eliezer about his father the first night at Birkenau. As time unfolds, Eliezer takes the ascendancy in the father-son relationship, making decisions, taking charge of their common welfare, even feeling angry at his father for not knowing how to avoid the Kapo's wrath and getting beaten: "That is what concentration camp life had made of me". Although he never abandons his father the way Rabbi Eliahou's son had, Eliezer has his mental moments of filial disloyalty and betrayal. When they are temporarily separated during an air alert at Buchenwald, Eliezer thinks "Don't let me find him! If only I could get rid of this dead weight", but he immediately feels ashamed. However, when his father is carried away to the crematory in the night, perhaps still alive, Eliezer must face the terrible truth: "And, in the depths of my being, in the recesses of my weakened conscience, could I have searched it, I might perhaps have found something like—free at last". He sees himself, then, as finally no better than Rabbi Eliahou's son.

Eliezer's Sense of Self

Just as Wiesel radically overturns the stock *Bildungsroman* pattern of master and apprentice, he alters the traditional process of the evolving self on its way to fulfillment. On the day of deportation, Eliezer looks back at his home where he had spent so many years "imagining what my life would be like". The ancient story of youth's departure from the nest, encountering the world and fleshing out the skeletal self, becomes for Eliezer a story of decomposing flesh, of becoming a skeleton. Literally overnight, Eliezer tells us, his sense of self evaporated: "The student of the Talmud, the child that I was, had been consumed in the flames. There remained only a shape that looked like me". Even the name for the "shape that looked like me" dissolves with the engraving of A-7713 on his left arm. The identity nurtured for twelve years collapses in one day.

Eliezer's sense of self is identical with his spiritual life. The worst of *Night*'s outrages, movingly worded by François Mauriac in the Foreword, is the "death of God in the soul of a child who suddenly discovers absolute evil". Again, the flames of the first night, fueled by the truckload of babies, "consumed my faith forever," "murdered my God and my soul and turned my dreams to dust". The two most powerful dramatizations of the consequences of Eliezer's sundered faith—the faith that had given richness and depth to his living—are the hanging of the boy and the first High Holy Days spent in Buna [concentration camp]. For Eliezer, God is "hanging here on this gallows". If God is not dead, then he deserves man's contempt, Eliezer feels. The bitterness pours forth during Rosh Hashanah and Yom Kippur with the mockery of the prisoners carrying out the forms, the absurdity of the starving debating whether to fast. While thousands pray, Eliezer offers up outraged accusations:

> But these men here, whom You have betrayed, whom You have allowed to be tortured, butchered, gassed, burned, what do they do? They pray before You! They praise Your name!

Like Huck Finn, Eliezer knows you can't pray a lie:

> My eyes were open and I was alone—terribly alone in a world without God and without man. Without love or

mercy. I had ceased to be anything but ashes, yet I felt myself to be stronger than the Almighty, to whom my life had
been tied for so long. I stood amid that praying congregation, observing it like a stranger.

Also in this scene of the praying ten thousand, one can see
Wiesel's ironic presentation of the community that the prepared initiate is to take his place in upon completion of ap-
prenticeship, the culmination of *Bildungsromane,* public and
ceremonial like the ordination of clergy or the commissioning
of officers. This is a congregation of the living dead, a community of corpses acting out a charade. This is as anti as a
Bildungsroman can get. Furthermore, if the Book of Exodus
can be described as a *Bildungsroman* on the level of an entire
people, *Night* can also be read as an anti-Exodus as [professor
of theology] Lawrence S. Cunningham has cogently argued:
"The life giving biblical myth of election, liberation, covenant,
and promise becomes the vehicle for telling the story of the
unnatural order of death-domination".

Loss of Faith in the Midst of Genocide

Irving Halperin

Irving Halperin was a professor emeritus of English and creative writing at San Francisco State University, where he was on the faculty for forty years. He died in 2000 at age seventy-eight. Halperin did extensive research on the Holocaust, culminating in two books based on that research.

According to Irving Halperin, Wiesel is a pious and devout young man, with full faith in the power of God to protect him and his Jewish community. But little by little, layer by layer, Wiesel's trust in God is peeled away amidst the genocidal horror perpetrated by the Nazis. He saw that conducting themselves as "good Jews" and remaining compliant, as was a tenet of their faith, did not save them from evil. In the excerpt below, Halperin also states that Wiesel's belief in the goodness of mankind is stripped away in the struggle for individual survival.

Night defines the nature and charts the consequences of a loss of faith in the protagonist, Eliezer, as incident by incident, layer by layer, his trust in God and man is peeled away. It is this "peeling down" process which constitutes the essential structure of *Night* and enables us to see it as a whole; the purpose of what follows is to adumbrate [outline] this process.

Eliezer as a boy in Sighet, a small town in Transylvania, absorbed the religious beliefs of his teacher, Moché the beadle, at a Hasidic synagogue. Moché prescribed that one should pray to God for "the strength to ask Him the right questions."

Irving Halperin, *Responses to Elie Wiesel: Critical Essays by Major Jewish and Christian Scholars*, New York: Persea Books, 1978. Copyright © 1978 by Persea Books, Inc. All rights reserved. Reproduced by permission.

"Man raises himself toward God by the questions he asks Him," he [Moché] was fond of repeating. "That is the true dialogue. Man questions God and God answers. But we don't understand His answers. We can't understand them. Because they come from the depths of the soul, and they stay there until death. You will find the true answers, Eliezer, only within yourself!"

Later, as a result of his experiences during the Holocaust, Eliezer would cease expecting to get answers to his questions; indeed, he would come to say that question and answer are not necessarily interrelated. Then what should men do—stop asking such questions? Not at all. The protagonists in [Wiesel's] later novels, in *The Town Beyond the Wall* and *The Gates of the Forest*, contend that men must continue to pose them. But not to God, who, in the eyes of the Wieselean narrator, remained silent during the Holocaust. Rather, these questions must come out of the depths of men and be addressed to other men. For to be human, to exercise one's humanity, is to go on posing such questions, even in the face of the Absurd, of Nothingness.

Eliezer Realizes Jews' Way of Life Did Not Protect Them

But such recognition for the protagonist was in the distant future. Meanwhile, in the beginning of *Night*, the boy Eliezer did not question Moché's teachings. He believed that as long as Jews studied and were pious no evil could touch them. The Germans proved he was mistaken when they occupied Sighet in the spring of 1944. In consequence, the first of Moché's teachings jettisoned by Eliezer was the notion that a Jew should live lowly, self-effacing and inconspicuous. Certainly Moché was an "invisible" man. The narrator says of him; "Nobody ever felt embarrassed by him. Nobody ever felt encumbered by his presence. He was a past master in the art of making himself insignificant, of seeming invisible."

And yet remaining "invisible" did not help Moché; the Germans systematically disposed of him along with Sighet's entire Jewish population. In the beginning of the Occupation, Jews were ordered to wear yellow stars, then they were driven out of their homes and herded into ghettos. A "Jewish council" and Jewish police were imposed on them. Some of the populace desperately attempted to escape annihilation by stationing themselves in such places and at such tasks that would keep them out of sight. And they further deluded themselves by thinking: The Germans—after all, this was the twentieth century—would oppress them up to a certain point and no further. So the popular advice was: Just do what they tell you; they only kill those who put up resistance. But in the end, packs on their backs, the Jewish community was marched off to a transport center, jammed into cattle wagons, and sent off to concentration camps. Meekness, staying "invisible," had not worked. And it is as though Wiesel laments that here was another instance wherein the Jew contributed to his agelong fate as victim and "specialist" in suffering. Ought not the time come when the Jew will make history itself tremble—when, if need be, *he* will be the executioner? In sum, Eliezer learned from having undergone the Occupation and deportation, that it is useless to employ the disguises of the "invisible" Jew. And this recognition constituted the first major puncture of his heretofore innocent faith in the teachings of Moché.

Flames of Auschwitz Consume Faith

Belief in God the fifteen-year-old Eliezer had before he came to Auschwitz [concentration camp]. But there, in *anus mundi* [anus of the world], that faith was consumed in the flames that consumed children. There "God" was the official on the train ramp who separated life from death with a flick of a finger to the right or left. Yet some Jews continued to urge children to pray to God. "You must never lose faith," they said to Eliezer, "even when the sword hangs over your head. That's the teaching of our sages."

But could the sages have imagined the limitless depravity of the Nazis? Could they, in all their wisdom, have counseled a boy of fifteen on how to react to the mass burning of children? To see a child's head, arms, and legs go up in flame—that is an indisputable fact, a measurable phenomenon.

Did He care that children were being consumed by fire? This is the question raised by the narrator of *Night*. And if He does nothing to prevent the mass murder of children. Eliezer cries out: "Why should I bless His name?" This outcry is the sign of, as François Mauriac says in his foreword to the book, "the death of God in the soul of a child who suddenly discovers absolute evil." And this breakdown of religious faith calls forth Eliezer's resolve "never to forget."

> Never shall I forget that night, the first night in camp, which has turned my life into one long night, seven times cursed and seven times sealed. Never shall I forget that smoke. Never shall I forget the little faces of the children, whose bodies I saw turned into wreaths of smoke beneath a silent blue sky.
>
> Never shall I forget those flames which consumed my faith forever.
>
> Never shall I forget that nocturnal silence which deprived me, for all eternity, of the desire to live. Never shall I forget those moments which murdered my God and my soul and turned my dreams to dust. Never shall I forget these things, even if I am condemned to live as long as God Himself. Never.

So, too, on the eve of Rosh Hashanah, Eliezer, who until then had always been devoted to this holiday, thinks, bitterly:

> Why, but why should I bless him? In every fiber I rebelled. Because He has had thousands of children burned in His pits? Because He kept six crematories working night and day, on Sundays and feast days? Because in His great might

He had created Auschwitz, Birkenau, Buna, and so many factories of death? How could I say to Him: "Blessed art Thou, Eternal, Master of the Universe, who chose us from among the races to be tortured day and night, to see our fathers, our mothers, our brothers, end in the crematory? Praised be Thy Holy Name, Thou Who hast chosen us to be butchered on Thine Altar?"

After Auschwitz, Eliezer could no longer speak of God's goodness or His ultimate purposes.

Loss of Faith Leads to World of Darkness

What is the immediate consequence of this loss of faith? Eliezer feels as though he were a lost soul condemned to wander in a haunted realm of darkness. Here the word "darkness" needs to be underscored, for it is a world at the poles from the one of "light" which Eliezer, as a student of the Cabbala [or kabbalah] and Talmud, inhabited in Sighet. By day the Talmud, and at night, by candlelight, he and his teacher Moché would study together, searching for "the revelation and mysteries of the cabbala." There was not only candlelight when they studied; the Talmud, the Zohar, the cabbalistic books themselves were light; they illuminated the nature of the "question" and suggested the answer; they seemed to draw Moché and Eliezer toward the shining realm of the eternal "where question and answer would become one."

But the light in *Night* is of brief duration; the atmosphere of the book is almost entirely that of blackness. The fires of Auschwitz consume the light, the religious faith, of Eliezer and leave him a "damned soul" wandering through a darkness where question and answer would *never* become one.

Myth of Civilized Society Shattered

What other kinds of disillusionment are experienced by Eliezer? I have already pointed out two—his realization that to be an "invisible" Jew did not protect one from the Nazis and, second, his turning away from God on witnessing the mass burning of children at Auschwitz. There was also his loss of faith in both the myth of twentieth-century civilized man and the tradition of the inviolable bonds between Jewish parents and children. Before coming to Auschwitz, Eliezer had believed that twentieth-century man was civilized. He had supposed that people would try to help one another in difficult times; certainly his father and teachers had taught him that every Jew is responsible for all other Jews. Until the gates of a concentration camp closed upon him he had no reason to doubt that the love between parents and children was characterized by sacrifice, selflessness, and utmost fealty.

But Auschwitz changed all that. There he was forced to look on while a young boy was tortured and then hanged—his death taking more than a half hour of "slow agony." There dozens of men fought and trampled one another for an extra ration of food. In one instance, he saw a son actually killing his elderly father over a portion of bread while other prisoners looked on indifferently. In Auschwitz the conduct of most prisoners was rarely selfless. Almost every man was out to save his own skin; and to do so he would steal, betray, buy life with the lives of others.

Eliezer's Own Conduct Causes Loss of Faith

Eliezer's progressive disillusionment did not come about simply because of what he witnessed in Auschwitz; he did not only observe the breakdown of faith; he himself in part caused it to happen. Consider Eliezer's thoughts and conduct with respect to his father when both were concentration camp prisoners. Eliezer feels that his father is an encumbrance, an albatross, who jeopardizes his own chances for survival. The son himself is ailing, emaciated, and in attempting to look after the older man strains his own limited physical resources. Moreover, such efforts make him dangerously conspicuous—always a perilous condition for concentration camp prisoners.

And yet he despises himself for not having lifted a hand when his elderly father was struck by a Kapo. He had looked on, thinking: "Yesterday I should have sunk my nails into the criminal's flesh. Have I changed so much, then?"

Eliezer's conflict of wanting to protect his father and, conversely, to be separated from him, is so desperate that when the father is on the verge of dying, the son feels ashamed to think: "If only I could get rid of this dead weight, so that I could use all my strength to struggle for my own survival, and only worry about myself." Again, when the dying man is struck with a truncheon by an officer, Eliezer, fearing to be beaten, stands still, like one paralyzed. Finally, when his father is taken off to the crematoria, the son cannot weep. Grief there is in him and yet he feels free of his burden. Thus another illusion is discarded by a boy who had been reared in a tradition that stresses loyalty and devotion to one's parents.

The death of his father leaves Eliezer in a state of numbness; he feels that nothing more can affect him. But there remains still another illusion he is to shed—the belief that on being liberated the prisoners would be capable of avenging themselves on the enemy. They had endured so much in order to live to the day of liberation. How often had the prisoners spoken to one another about what they would do to the Germans. And yet when Buchenwald is liberated, Eliezer observes with anger and disgust that his fellow prisoners are concerned only with bread and not revenge.

He has lost not only his father but also faith in God and humanity. Many of his previously untested beliefs in the staying powers of the "invisible" Jew, the unquestionable justice of God, the built-in restraints of twentieth-century civilization, and the enduring strength of familial bonds between Jewish parents and children have been peeled away. He will have to journey for a long time and through many lands before arriving at that point of retrospective clarity when he can even first frame the "right questions" concerning his season in hell. He will need to stand before some "false" gates before he can turn away from them. And yet, all through this time, he is to hold fast to the belief that his teacher Moché instilled in him: that there *is* an "orchard of truth," and that for entering the gate to this place every human being has his own key. One function of the Wieselean novels that follow *Night* is to trace the protagonist-survivor's journey in search of such a gate.

Holocaust Victims Could Not Fathom the Reality of the Holocaust

Michael Berenbaum

Michael Berenbaum has authored and edited sixteen books and is a noted authority on the Holocaust. He is a lecturer and an adjunct professor of theology at the University of Judaism in Los Angeles. He is also involved in producing films about the Holocaust that have won Academy and Emmy awards, among other recognitions.

Elie Wiesel, in Michael Berenbaum's assessment, expresses impatience with the "business as usual" outlook of his community prior to their deportation to the death camps. The traditions and education of the Sighet community members did not prepare them to accept the reality of their situation and take action. Even the existing inmates at the Auschwitz concentration camp are shocked by the self-delusion evinced by the new arrivals. Wiesel, says Berenbaum, refuses to deify the victims, revealing all of their human behaviors and weaknesses.

Wiesel's novels reveal the weakness, as well as the strength, of people under the strain of extraordinary conditions, and Wiesel's tone is often highly critical. In fact, [psychologist and author Bruno] Bettelheim could point to Wiesel's novels, and most particularly to his memoir *Night*, to substantiate some of his own claims. In reality Wiesel's defense of the mystery of the Holocaust is but another confession of the void. Wiesel's assertion of the mystery preserves for the reader the holiness of the victims precisely at the point that Wiesel's

Michael Berenbaum, *Responses to Elie Wiesel: Critical Essays by Major Jewish and Christian Scholars*, New York: Persea Books, 1978. Copyright © 1978 by Michael Berenbaum. Reproduced by permission.

writings underscore the compromises which were made. Wiesel's differences with [German Jewish political theorist Hannah] Arendt and Bettelheim closely resemble the differences outlined between Wiesel and [writer Richard] Rubenstein; namely, that like most of the American Jewish community, Wiesel is uncomfortable with the use of analytic language, the abandonment of the mythic, symbolic system of traditional Judaism. Wiesel is troubled by the use of language that does not preserve the complexity of the original experience and that ignores its nuances and ambiguities. Furthermore, Wiesel sees the collapse of one world view and chronicles its demise while he feels acute discomfort when others, who share his perceptions but do not openly manifest his pain, confront him with the reality they both perceive. . . .

Elie Wiesel has claimed that he has written directly of the Holocaust only in *Night*; and it is in his memoir *Night* that Wiesel expresses his greatest impatience with the "business as usual" attitude which predominated his community. Wiesel wrote that in the spring of 1944, "people were interested in everything—in strategy, in diplomacy, in politics, in Zionism—but not in their own fate." In his description of Sighet, he commented that even after the Nazis had arrived and the verdict had been pronounced, "the Jews of Sighet continued to smile." Wiesel's imagery reflects his impatience with skepticism with which his warning is greeted. In *Night* the character is Moshe the beadle. In an "Evening Guest" the character is Elijah who brings evil tidings of doom rather than good tidings of the coming Messiah. The messages are never heeded. Wiesel, like Bettelheim, is critical of the Jewish community's failure to confront the reality and act accordingly.

Just as Bettelheim points to [Holocaust victim] Anne Frank's education as an example of dysfunctional denial, Wiesel portrays characters whose education is similarly inappropriate to their situation. . . . Eliezer was trained for eternity as history abruptly intruded into his life. . . .

Prisoners of the Buchenwald Concentration Camp standing at call in their civilian clothes, Germany. USHMM Photo Archives.

The degree of self-delusion is even a shock to the inmates who can no longer accept the blindness of the outside world. In *Night* Wiesel describes the impatience with which the new arrivals at Auschwitz were greeted. The inmates cannot believe that the world does not yet know and that people can still be arriving complacently for their own cremation. Wiesel continues to be critical of the Jews' repression of their fate. He described his family's decision not to uproot themselves and emigrate to Palestine and then immediately described the observance of Passover which commemorates the Israelites' departure from Egypt in the middle of the night without sufficient time for their bread to rise. Just prior to the description of the Passover seder, Shlomo Wiesel comments:

> "I'm too old, my son . . . I'm too old to start a new life. I'm too old to start from scratch again . . ."

Ironically, Shlomo Wiesel renounces the possibility of a new life just as he celebrates the festival of spring. On the seventh day of Passover, Jews commemorate the saving at the sea and the "Song of the Sea" is chanted in the synagogue. According to Wiesel's description in *Night*, it was precisely on the seventh day that the Jewish leaders of Sighet were arrested. The remembrance of God's saving presence and the faith that God will continue to save His people falsely consoled the people and contributed to their illusions. The race toward death had begun, yet Wiesel observed:

> The general opinion was that we were going to remain in the ghetto until the end of the war, until the arrival of the Red Army. Then everything would be as before. *It was neither German nor Jew who ruled the ghetto—it was illusion.* (italics added)

Foremost among the illusions was the illusion of time.

Throughout Wiesel's novels and short stories a character continually reappears who has been to the camps and seen their reality and returns to the world of the living only to be frustrated by the victims for various other reasons. For example, the young arrivals at the camps wish to revolt, yet their elders reply, "One must never lose faith even when the sword hangs over your head. That's the teaching of our sages." Wiesel's tone here emphasizes the delusionary and debilitating nature of their faith.

[Historian] Lucy Dawidowicz in *The War Against the Jews* approaches Jewish behavior during the Holocaust from the perspective of Jewish sources. She spoke of the importance of Jewish tradition which emphasized the justice and goodness of what happened and taught that all must be accepted as good from God. The Jews saw themselves as co-workers with God and hence they responded with activity to impending danger developing the virtues "of self discipline, prudence, moderation, foregoing present gratification for eventual benefit." They found ways of circumventing discrimination and deflecting persecution. It was these methods that the Jews practiced during the Holocaust. Jewish policy had a double thrust. Internal Jewish policy was aimed at bolstering morale, outwardly alleviating hardship, and mullifying persecution. Although Dawidowicz does not deal with the concentration camp situation except for but the briefest references, the policies of the Jewish organizations are accurately described though not evaluated by her. The early Wiesel, the author of *Night*, felt that the bolstering of morale was a costly self-deception for the Jews while Bettelheim could easily see in Dawidowicz's descriptive documentation of the persistence of a business as usual attitude among the Jews. As Dawidowicz clearly shows, the nomos [normal rules and forms of a society], of the community re-established itself against quite quickly despite the anomic situation.

Wiesel does not shrink from exposing or at least uplifting aspects of the victims' behavior and refuses to unequivocally heroize the victims. In *Night* Wiesel describes the moments of anomie [lack of identity or ethical values] in which each man battled on his own for survival. The moments were the ones in which fathers betrayed sons and sons fathers. Rabbi Eliahou's son ran away from his father, and Eliezer resented the burden of his father's presence and briefly betrayed him. Wiesel continually underscores the price paid for survival both in terms of what has been called survivors' guilt and in terms of the knowledge of one's limited humanity. Wiesel describes his reaction to the death of his father:

> I did not weep, and it pained me that I could not weep. But I had no more tears. And, in the depths of my being, in the recesses of my weakened conscience, could I have searched it, I might perhaps have found something like—free at last.

Eliezer was freed of the burden of his father, but he was also bereft of his father's love. During the next months he lived as if in a haze without reason and without hope, consumed by his own guilt and the memory of betrayal. The tale of *Night* is a tale of fratricide and patricide as well as a tale of filial love and devotion. The moments of betrayal predominate, but there are also moments of triumph, moments when the young boy chooses death over betrayal, or when the condemned man proclaims "Long live liberty! A curse on Germany! A curse ..." The complexity of the picture that Wiesel presents forces the reader to confront the nuances of meaning, meaning that Wiesel fears might be lost in abstractions.

Reports of Genocide Threatened the Sighet Community's Definition of Itself

Ora Avni

Ora Avni is a professor of nineteenth- and twentieth-century French literature at Yale University.

When Moshe Beadle, a key figure in the beginning of Night, *escapes a deportation convoy and returns to Sighet to warn the community about the murder of his fellow deportees, he is met with disbelief. In the following selection, Ora Avni proposes that the self-positioning of both the teller and the listeners impacted their reactions to the information. The townspeople refused to believe Beadle's story, Avni states, because they would have to acknowledge its effect on them. The "narrative" they were born and immersed in could not accommodate Beadle's new, dismal view of humanity. Simultaneously, Moshe sought validation and acceptance for his story as a bridge to help him assimilate back into the community.*

Night is the story of a young boy's journey through hell, as he is taken first to a ghetto, and then to Auschwitz and Buchenwald [concentration camps]. . . .

Its opening focuses not so much on the boy, however, as on a foreigner, Moshe the Beadle, a wretched yet good-natured and lovable dreamer, versed in Jewish mysticism. When the town's foreign Jews are deported by the Nazis to an unknown destination, he leaves with them; but he comes back. Having miraculously survived the murder of his convoy, he hurries back to warn the others. No longer singing, humming, or praying, he plods from door to door, desperately repeating the same stories of calm and dispassionate killings. But, despite his unrelenting efforts, "people refused not only to believe his stories, but even to listen to them".

First Accounts of Atrocities Were Not Believed

Like Moshe the Beadle, the first survivors who told their stories either to other Jews or to the world were usually met with disbelief. When the first escapees from Ponar's killing grounds [a site in Lithuania where Nazis executed thousands of Jews] tried to warn the Vilna ghetto that they were not sent to work but to be murdered, not only did the Jews not believe them, but they accused the survivors of demoralizing the ghetto, and demanded that they stop spreading such stories: Similarly, when Jan Karski, the courier of the Polish government-in-exile who had smuggled himself into the Warsaw Ghetto so that he could report the Nazi's atrocities as an eyewitness, made his report to Justice Felix Frankfurter, the latter simply said, "I don't believe you." Asked to explain, he added, "I did not say that this young man is lying. I said I cannot believe him. There is a difference." How are we to understand this disbelief? What are its causes and effects, and above all, what lesson can we learn from it?. . .

On the one hand, Moshe's distress is undoubtedly Wiesel's. Like Moshe, Wiesel came back; like Moshe, he told his story; and like Moshe, he told it again and again. It is therefore not merely a question of informing others (for information purposes, once the story is told, one need not tell it again). Like Moshe, Wiesel clearly does not set out to impart information only, but to *tell the tale*, that is, to share a scene of narration with a community of readers. This explains why, while the *Shoah* [Holocaust] is in fact the subject of all his texts, Wiesel, wiser than Moshe, never recounted his actual experience in the death camps again. Like the opening episode of *Night*, his other works deal with "before" and "after": before, as a premonition of things to come; after, as a call for latecomers to see themselves accountable for living in a post-*Shoah* world. . . .

Self-Positioning of Narrator and Listener Are Key

To what, then, does this episode owe its exemplary value? Why has Moshe, the ultimate *Shoah* survivor-narrator, come back? Why does he feel compelled to endlessly repeat his story? Why does he no longer pray? On the other hand, why are his listeners so recalcitrant? Why do they not believe him? Why do they accuse him of madness or of ulterior motives? Why do they all but gag him? That this episode illustrates widespread attitudes towards all accounts of Nazi atrocities and Jewish victimization is unquestionable. We shall therefore focus on the *self-positioning* of the subject (teller or listener, knowledgeable or uninformed) in the face of accounts of the *Shoah*, be it at the dinner table, in the classroom, on the psychoanalyst's couch, in academe, or in the morning paper. It is at once a positioning vis-à-vis one's self, one's interlocutors, and one's community. . . .

Our critique of the psychoanalytic approach relies on our view of the subject's self-positioning in history, at once in the privacy of his inner world, in the limited exchange set with one's interlocutor (say, a therapist), and mostly, in the larger context of stories we tell ourselves versus stories into which we are born. The exemplary value of *Night*'s opening episode hinges upon its containing the narrative of the boy, and by extension of any survivor, within the problems raised by this self-positioning.

Prior to his own encounter with Nazism, the boy asks Moshe: "Why are you so anxious that people should believe what you say? In your place, I shouldn't care whether they believe me or not. . ." Indeed, in comparison with the ordeal from which he has just escaped, there seems to be little reason for Moshe's present distress. What, then, hangs upon the credibility of his story? Why do the town people refuse to listen to the beadle? What effect does their reaction have on the *project* that brought him back to town? Somehow tentatively, Moshe answers the boy's query:

> "You don't understand," he said in despair. "You can't understand. I have been saved miraculously. I managed to get back here. Where did I get the strength from? I wanted to come back to Sighet to tell you the story of my death. So that you could prepare yourselves while there was still time. To live? I don't attach any importance to my life any more. I'm alone. No, I wanted to come back, and to warn you. And see how it is, no one will listen to me. . . ."

Moshe Tries to Impose Coherence on Trauma Story

Moshe's anguished insistence on being heard undoubtedly illustrates the well-known recourse to narrative in order to impose coherence on an incoherent experience (a commonplace of literary criticism), to work through a trauma (a commonplace of psychoanalysis), the laudable drive to testify to a crime (a commonplace of *Shoah* narratives), or even the heroics of saving others (a commonplace of resistance literature). Although such readings of *Night* are certainly not irrelevant, I do not think that they do justice to the gripping urgency of his unwelcome and redundant narrative, unless we read the text literally: Moshe came back "to tell you the story."

We must rule out simply imparting knowledge, since Moshe's undertaking clearly does not stop at communicating the story. A scenario in which the town folks gather around him to listen to his story, and then go on about their business would be absurd. In this case, to "believe" the story is to be affected by it. . . .

Moshe came back to town in order to tell his story, and if indeed he is determined to secure the felicitous uptake of his narrative's illocutionary force, then this determination reveals yet *another project*, one that is even more exacting in that it affects his (and his fellow villagers') being-in-the-world: his return to town is also an attempt to reaffirm his ties to his community (its conventions, its values), to reintegrate into the human community of his past—a community whose integrity was put into question by the absurd, incomprehensible, and unassimilable killings he had witnessed. Through his encounter with Nazism, Moshe has witnessed not only the slaughter of a human cargo, but the demise of his notion of humanity—a notion, however, still shared by the town folks. As long as they hold on to this notion of humanity to which he can no longer adhere, he is, *ipso facto*, a freak. Coming back to town to tell his story to a receptive audience is therefore Moshe's way back to normalcy, back to humanity. Only by having a community integrate his dehumanizing experience into the narratives of self-representation that it shares and infer a new code of behavior based on the information he is imparting, only by becoming part of this community's history, can Moshe hope to reclaim his lost humanity (the question remains, as we shall see, at what price to that community). It is therefore not a question of privately telling the story (to oneself, to one's editor or to one's analyst) as of having others—a whole community—*claim* it, *appropriate* it, and *react* (properly) to it. . . .

Moshe and Town People Have Different Needs

Night's opening episode thus raises two major questions, stretched over the two ends of the communication process: Why did Moshe so desperately need to be listened to; and why do the town folks obtusely refuse to take in his story (at the risk of their lives)? Clearly, something crucial must be at stake for both parties, something that defies storytelling, "lifting to consciousness," or literalized metaphors. Whether we address the question from one end of the scene of narration or from the other, I suggest that the answer is one and the same.

We may approach it through two often-overlooked truisms: on the one hand, whatever horrible trauma an individual may have experienced, he or she remains an individual, no more, no less. That person will retain and exercise all or any of the psychological and psychoanalytic processes by which one normally sorts out experiences or fantasies. So much for the idiosyncratic treatment of psychic traces, however, since, as we have seen, no individual lives in a vacuum. Our second truism is, therefore, that we live in society, that is, we are born into a world in which our options are predetermined and limited: we are born into an already existing language, into social, ethical and legal codes; we are born into a world rife with events, narratives, histories—in short, *memories*—which are as constitutive of our selves as are our fantasies or experiences. Moreover, as education and the media have tightened their grip on our lives, societies have become increasingly permeable to each other; we share more stories, more myths, more histories than ever before. . . .

Now, the dynamics of *Night*'s opening episode may be clearer: Moshe and the town folks occupy two opposite ends of a transaction. Moshe wants the community to assimilate his story, to take it in and learn its lesson, in the hope that it will allow him a way out of the unbearable solitude into which his experience has cast him, and bridge over the tear that his encounter with the dispassionate force of evil has introduced in his life. In other words, he wants the agrammaticality of his experience, his odd and deviant *parole* to become part of their *langue* [linguistic system shared by a community]. The town folk, however, do not want to take up this horror, to make it theirs, to make this story the *rallying point* between themselves and the narrator, since if they did, his burden would become theirs: it would then behoove *them* to mend the tear, and to assimilate an unassimilable experience (an experience that is not, but would become, theirs, should they be forced into a shared scene of narration with Moshe). To integrate Moshe's *parole* into their *langue* would demand such an extensive review of the rules of the *langue* by which they live that it could put its very structure and coherence in question. They would rather risk their lives than tamper with their cognitive framework. Moshe's compulsion can thus be understood only within the dynamics of his interaction with his community, just as the denial of each member of the community can only be understood as an attempt to maintain the integrity of this community. . . .

It has often been said that *Night* is the gloomy story of a loss for which no solace, no solution is offered. Indeed, "Elie Wiesel has repeatedly stated that survivors of the Holocaust live in a nightmare world that can never be understood. . . ." But it should also be noted that, although *Night* is the only novel in which he dealt directly and explicitly with his experience of the *Shoah*, Wiesel's whole life has been dedicated to its ensuing moral and historical imperatives. Moshe the Beadle (Wiesel's spokesman) thus offers a critique of facile answers to post-*Shoah* difficulties—narrowly individualized answers that, despite their limited usefulness, nonetheless overlook the collective dimension and its impact on the individual's self-positioning. Excessive separateness of past and present is yet another form of repression, another defense mechanism.

Wiesel Uses *Night* as a Metaphor for the Horror of Genocide

Ellen S. Fine

Ellen S. Fine is a literary critic.

Night is an appropriate metaphor for the darkness and evil of the Holocaust and the darkness that overtakes the human spirit in the death camps, states Ellen S. Fine in the following excerpt. The prisoners in the concentration camps live as if they were already dead, constantly aware of the Nazis' ability to exterminate them at any moment. Further, time and a sense of night and day are obliterated in the camp and during transport in crowded cattle cars. And, as Fine points out, the deadly march from the Buna concentration camp to the Buchenwald camp occurs in the blackness of freezing winds and snow. The final descent into night occurs when Wiesel awakens to discover that his father was removed from his quarters during the night, taking Wiesel to a psychologically impenetrable darkness.

The theme of night pervades Elie Wiesel's memoir as suggested by the title itself, which encompasses the overall Holocaust landscape—*l'univers concentrationnaire*—a world synonymous with methodical brutality and radical evil. The dark country presented to us is self-contained and self-structured, governed by its own criminal gods who have created laws based upon a death-dominated ideology. Wiesel uses the word *Night* throughout his writing to denote this strange sphere, unreal and unimaginable in its otherworldliness....

Ellen S. Fine, *Legacy of Night: The Literary Universe of Elie Wiesel*, Albany: State University of New York Press, 1982. Copyright © 1982 State University of New York. Reproduced by permission of the State University of New York Press.

Eliezer's World Is Defined by Night

Eliezer, the narrator of the book, is, in effect, a child of the Night, who relates the journey from the friendly Jewish community tucked away in the mountains of Transylvania to Auschwitz [concentration camp]—the frightening and foreign capital of the kingdom of Night. During the course of the trip certain events take place which stand out in the narrator's memory and often occur during the nocturnal hours. The theme of night is linked to the passage of time in the account itself. Within the larger framework, more specific phases, characterized by the motifs of the *first* and *last* night, structure the descent into terror and madness, and point to the demarcations between the known and unknown.

Once Eliezer enters Auschwitz, he loses his sense of time and reality. Darkness envelops him and penetrates within: his spirit is shrouded, his God eclipsed, the blackness eternal. Pushed to his limits, the narrator experiences the *other* haunted and interminable night. . . . The intermingling of particular nights with Night, the measuring of time alongside timelessness, corresponds to a style that interweaves a direct narration of events with subtle reflections upon the experience.

In 1941, when the narrative begins, Eliezer is a deeply Orthodox boy of twelve, living in the town of Sighet, situated on the Hungarian-Rumanian border. The word *night* is first mentioned with regard to his evening visits to the synagogue: "During the day I studied the Talmud, and at night I ran to the synagogue to weep over the destruction of the Temple". While this nocturnal lamentation is part of a religious tradition, its prominent position in the text can be interpreted as a prediction of the bleak shadow cast upon Jewish communities throughout twentieth-century Europe.

Eliezer spends many of his evenings in the semidarkness of the synagogue where half-burned candles flicker as he converses with Moché, his chosen master of the Kabbala [or Kab-

Soldiers burying bodies in a pit at Belzec Concentration Camp in Poland, circa 1942.
Photo by Imagno/Getty Images.

balah]; they exchange ideas about the nature of God, man, mysticism, and faith. Night, here, exudes a poetic and pious atmosphere as the time for prayer, interrogation and dialogue within the context of the secure and the traditional. Indeed, the narrator's experience of benevolent night begins to change with Moché's expulsion from Sighet. Deported because he is a foreign Jew, Moché is sent to [Lithuania], driven to a forest [the Ponar killing grounds] along with hundreds of other Jews, and shot in front of freshly dug pits. Wounded in the leg only, he rises from the mass grave and miraculously makes his way back to Sighet to recount what he calls "the story of my own death." "Jews, listen to me," he cries out. "It's all I ask of you, I don't want money or pity. Only listen to me". No one in the *shtetl*, including Eliezer, believes his tale, and Moché is forced into silence, Wiesel's first example of the unheeded witness whose futile warnings predict the fate of the entire Jewish community. This occurs towards the end of 1942.

Nazis Were Skilled at Deceptive Calm

Without being explicit, Wiesel's narrative closely follows the historical events that led to the expulsion of the Hungarian Jews. The years 1942 and 1943 as rapidly described in the text were fairly normal for the Jews of Sighet. While anti-Jewish legislation was enacted and periods of calm alternated with those of turbulence, day still predominated over night. From 1938 to 1944, Hungarian prime ministers ranged from eager collaborators to those who collaborated reluctantly, resulting, in cycles of despair and hope for the Jews who were unable to assess their situation realistically. In 1944 the Jewish community of Hungary was the only large group still intact. The circumstances changed drastically, however, in March, with the German takeover of the country and the installation of the pro-German Sztójay government. Adolf Eichmann, commander of the Special Action Unit . . . came to Hungary to personally carry out one of the most concentrated and systematic destruction operations in Europe. In the spring of 1944, with the end of the war in sight, the Nazis deported and eventually wiped out 450,000 Jews, 70 percent of the Jews of Greater Hungary. The Jews from the Carpathian region and Transylvania were among the first to be ghettoized and then rounded up. Of the fifteen thousand Jews in Sighet's community alone, about fifty families survived.

The Germans were notorious for their methods of deceiving their victims by dispelling notions of fear and creating the illusion of normality as they went about setting the machinery of extermination in motion. Eliezer speaks of life returning to normal, even after the Nazis forced the Jews of Sighet into two ghettos fenced off from the rest of the population by barbed wire. At least, he remarks, Jews were living among their brothers and the atmosphere was somewhat peaceful. This deceptively secure setting was soon to be shattered.

"Night fell," says the narrator, describing an evening gathering of friends in the courtyard of his family's house in the large ghetto. A group of about twenty was listening attentively to tales told by his father, when suddenly a Jewish policeman entered and interrupted his father's story, summoning him to an emergency session of the Jewish council. "The good story he had been in the middle of telling us was to remain unfinished," Eliezer notes. . . .

Night Becomes Time of Fire, Silence, and Death

Suspended in the midst of its natural flow, the father's story is a metaphor for Jewish life and lives abruptly brought to a standstill in the middle of the *night*. When the father returns at midnight from the council meeting, he announces news of the deportation to be held the following day.

From this point on, time is defined by the first and last night. Eliezer refers to "our last night at home," spent in the large ghetto after watching the first transport of victims parade through the streets under the blazing sun, the infernal counterpart to Night. Then, there is the last evening in the small ghetto, where Eliezer, his parents, and three sisters observe the traditional Sabbath meal: "We were, we felt, gathered for the last time round the family table. I spent the night turning over thoughts and memories in my mind, unable to find sleep".

Expelled from the small ghetto, Eliezer and his family, along with other members of the community, are thrown into cattle cars where they endure three long nights. Day is left far behind. The theme of night corresponds here to the reduction of space. Whereas the gentle gloom of the synagogue provided the framework for a boundless exploration of sacred doctrines, the ghetto period—in its progression from larger to smaller—serves as a transitional space, leading to the nailed-up doors of the cattle wagons, which plunge the prisoners into the confinement and extreme darkness of a night without limits.

The night of the cattle wagons is hallucinatory. Madame Schächter, a woman of fifty, who along with her ten-year-old son had been deported separately from her husband and two elder sons, starts to go mad. On the third and last night in the train, she screams out as if possessed by an evil spirit, conjuring up vivid images of fire and a furnace. Some of the men peer through the barred train window to see what Madame Schächter is pointing to, but all they can glimpse is blackness. Night is both within and without, surrounding the mad prophet who continuously cries out, as if to predict the end of the world, but who is forcefully silenced by those around her who do not want to believe in the foreboding signs. At the terminus, Birkenau—Auschwitz, Madame Schächter gives one last howl: "Jews, look! Look through the window! Flames! Look!" As the train stops, the victims, in disbelief, observe red flames gushing out of the chimney into the black sky.

The theme of fire is present, indeed, throughout the text, from the half-burned candles of the synagogue, where Eliezer and Moché attempt to illuminate the mysteries of the universe, to the relentless sun of the ghetto liquidation, culminating in the savage blaze of the death pits and crematoria. "Here the word 'furnace' was not a word empty of meaning," the narrator notes, "it floated on the air, mingling with the smoke. It was perhaps the only word which did have any real meaning here". Fire is, indeed, an integral part of Night, as suggested by the term *Holocaust* itself, which signifies widespread destruction by fire or a sacrificial burnt offering.

When Eliezer sees the vivid flames leaping out of a ditch where little children are being burned alive, he pinches his face in order to know if he is awake or dreaming in this nightmarish atmosphere of "Hell *made immanent*." The young boy watches babies thrown into the smouldering pits and people all around murmuring *Kaddish* (the Jewish prayer for the dead) for themselves—the living dead—as they slowly move in a kind of *danse macabre*. They give the eerie impression that they are participating in their own funeral. For a moment, the narrator contemplates throwing himself on the barbed wire, but the instinct for survival prevails. As he enters the Holocaust kingdom on that first night he recites a ritualistic incantation, which marks his initiation into one long and never-ending night and commits him to remember it always:

> Never shall I forget that night, the first night in camp, which has turned my life into one long night, seven times cursed and seven times sealed. Never shall I forget that smoke. Never shall I forget the little faces of the children, whose bodies I saw turned into wreaths of smoke beneath a silent blue sky.
>
> Never shall I forget those flames which consumed my faith forever.
>
> Never shall I forget that nocturnal silence which deprived me, for all eternity, to the desire to live. Never shall I forget those moments which murdered my God and my soul and turned my dreams to dust. Never shall I forget these things, even if I am condemned to live as long as God Himself. Never.

This invocation summarizes the principal themes of Wiesel's first book, joining the theme of night to those of fire, silence, and the death of children, of God, and of the self. The moment of arrival designates the end of the reality-oriented structure of "outer" night, and the shift to "inner" night, in which time is suspended. As dawn breaks Eliezer observes: "So much had happened within such a few hours that I had lost all sense of time. When had we left our houses? And the ghetto? And the train? Was it only a week? One night—*one single night?* . . . Surely it was a dream".

Night Extinguishes Sense of Time

Indeed, like a dream sequence, the events of the camp journey have been accelerated and condensed into a short interval. "One of the most astonishing things," says Wiesel, "was that we lost all sense not only of time in the French meaning of the word, of *durée*, but even in the concept of years. . . . The ten-year-old boy and the sixty-year-old man not only looked alike, felt alike and lived alike, but walked alike. There was a certain 'levelling.'". . .

The concept of time that governs life in normal conditions thus changes radically in the concentrationary universe. But even more important than time is the highly organized and methodological procedure that deprives an individual of his humanness and transforms him into a thing while still alive. The *défaite du moi*, the "dissolution of the self," is the worst kind of living death and is a recurring theme in Holocaust literature.

After one single night in Auschwitz, Eliezer is turned into a subhuman, identified only by an anonymous number. Yesterday an active member of a community imbued with religious teachings and traditions, the boy is now bereft of all faith. A black flame, the demonic union of fire and night, has permeated his psyche. At the center of his soul lies a void:

> I too had become a completely different person. The student of the Talmud, the child that I was, had been consumed in the flames. There remained only a shape that looked like me. A dark flame had entered into my soul and devoured it.

On the eve of Rosh Hashanah, the last night of the Jewish year, Eliezer experiences a deep sense of alienation as he stands among his praying and sobbing compatriots who are observing the holiday. The once fervent youth is now a spectator of himself, a stranger to his beliefs, and in revolt against an absent God who has betrayed his people by allowing them to be tortured, gassed, and burned. "I was the accuser, God the accused. My eyes were open and I was alone—terribly alone in a world without God and without man". With blunted senses and branded flesh, the child turns away from his God and his heritage. His spirit is arrested in the confines of Night: the empire of darkness has taken possession of his inner being. For the boy of fifteen history has stopped.

Although time is essentially abolished in the kingdom of death, the narrator nevertheless continues to structure outer reality in the account itself by noting the nights that mark the principal stages of the trip. After three weeks in Auschwitz, he and his father are sent in a work transport to Buna, where they spend several weeks. The Germans finally evacuate the camp as Russian troops approach. Before the long cold voyage to Buchenwald, Eliezer meditates on the motif of *the last night*:

> The last night in Buna. Yet another last night. The last night at home, the last night in the ghetto, the last night in the train, and, now, the last night in Buna. How much longer were our lives to be dragged out from one 'last night' to another?

The march from Buna to Buchenwald takes place in blackness, amid glacial winds and falling snow. The boy realizes that the night he is leaving will be replaced by one even more unfathomable on the other side; the *invisible darkness* of the tomb. As the procession winds its way through the thick snow, numerous corpses are strewn upon its trail. After several days without food or water, the remaining prisoners are thrown into open cattle cars and transported to Buchenwald. For the starved skeletons who speed through the frozen landscape, "days were like nights and the nights left the dregs of their darkness in our souls". Suddenly, on the last day of this seemingly endless journey, a fierce cry rises up from among the inert bodies of the entire convoy—a collective death rattle that seems to emanate from beyond the grave. This shared song of death when no hope is left is a protest to the world which has abandoned them. A brutal expression of the agony of those who have reached their limits, this massive convulsion *is* the primeval language of Night. Finally, late in the evening, twelve survivors out of the hundred who started out reach Buchenwald.

The last night—and the most significant—is January 28, 1945. Eliezer's father, sick with dysentery, his head bloody from the blows of an SS guard, lies curled up miserably on his bunk bed. When his son awakens the next day, he realizes that his father has been carted away before dawn—perhaps still alive. It is the finality of this moment that virtually ends the narrative, plunging Eliezer into a realm where no light penetrates and where on some level, the *child of Night* remains for the rest of his life.

Victims of Genocide Can Lose Their Own Humanity

Ted L. Estess

Ted L. Estess is a professor of English and a member of the Honors College faculty at the University of Houston, Texas, where he has taught since 1977.

Ted L. Estess notes in the following selection that devotion to God and family are critical for Elie Wiesel. Wiesel is challenged to maintain his sense of decency, primarily as it relates to loyalty to his father. He vows not to lower himself to the level of other prisoners who put their own survival above that of their family members. However, Wiesel feels guilty for wishing his father was not a burden. Wiesel awakens one morning to find his father gone, spirited away in the night, to an almost certain fate. Estess states that suffering and horror stripped many inmates of their humanity and corrupted their souls. According to Estess, Wiesel's own awareness that he was capable of disregarding his own father is a final and devastating blow.

Night records how the Holocaust poisoned and nearly destroyed all primary relationships in Eliezer's life. His relationship to himself—and by this is meant his understanding of himself—is called into question on the first night at Auschwitz [concentration camp]. He says:

> The student of the Talmud, the child I was, had been consumed in the flames. There remained only a shape that looked like me. A dark flame had entered into my soul and devoured it. . . .

Devotion to His Father Becomes Crucial Human Tie

While his relationships to himself and to God are crucial for Eliezer, his relationship to his father is important as well. Through much of his time in the death camps this relationship remains the single tie to his life in Sighet. Just as Eliezer's relationship with God is the center of the religious dimension of the story, his relationship with his father is the center of the psychological quandary. To Wiesel, the two relationships are intrinsically connected, but they are not reducible to each other. They are distinct, each with its own integrity and its own significance. Both add focus to Eliezer's identity, so that the loss of either is psychically disturbing, and the loss of both altogether devastating.

The tenacity with which Eliezer clings to his father reflects an effort to draw back from the abyss that opens up with the loss of all human ties. The relationship functions as a touchstone to which Eliezer (and the entire narrative) returns again and again. He measures what is happening within himself in terms of what is happening in his relationship with his father. If he can sustain his unconditional commitment to his father, then something might abide in a world in which all is changing. Since anything can suddenly be taken away from the inmates of the death camps, Eliezer makes only one thing necessary to him: absolute fidelity to his father. God has broken His promises to His people; Eliezer, in contrast, determines ever more resolutely not to violate his covenant with his father.

Depravity of Auschwitz Drives Betrayals

Eliezer's struggle to maintain decency in his principal relationships finally focuses on this question: Will he betray his father and choose his own life at his father's expense? Eliezer watches one young man kill his father for a piece of bread; he sees another, Rabbi Eliahou's son, run off and leave his father in the snow. Gathering the last particles of outrage he possesses,

Eliezer prays to a God whom he no longer trusts: "My God, Lord of the Universe, give me strength never to do what Rabbi Eliahou's son has done."

After the long journey to Buchenwald [concentration camp], Eliezer's complex relationship to his father reaches its culmination. Seeing that Eliezer's struggle to keep his father alive is depleting his meager energy, the head of the block counsels him:

> Listen to me, boy. Don't forget that you're in a concentration camp. Here, every man has to fight for himself and not think of anyone else. Even of his father. Here, there are no fathers, no brothers, no friends. Everyone lives and dies for himself alone.

In response, Eliezer reflects: "He was right, I thought in the most secret region of my heart, but I dared not admit it." Eliezer continues to struggle against what he considers to be the final debasement of his humanity: to choose himself over his father. But when his father dies, Eliezer makes this disturbing admission:

> And, in the depths of my being, in the recesses of my weakened conscience, could I have searched it, I might perhaps have found something like—free at last!

Choosing Himself

With this event the concentration camp has worked its horror completely in the boy's soul. In his view, he is guilty of having acquiesced in his father's death. The reader is likely to pity Eliezer, but Eliezer asks for no sympathy. In disclosing his feelings, Eliezer simply confesses the extent to which the Holocaust has corrupted the primary relationships of life. In stripping away a person's past, in pushing him to the limits of his physical endurance, in reversing all the expectations he had of man and God—in all these ways life in the camps forced the victim to choose himself without regard for the other. "At that moment," Eliezer sadly admits, "what did the others matter!"

Here Wiesel displays the effect of suffering on the soul of the victim. He refuses to sentimentalize or legitimate undeserved suffering by bestowing on it some healing or expiatory power or by pretending that suffering of itself ennobles the human spirit. People respond differently to suffering: some hold intact their previous world views, some become angry and finally despair, some transform suffering into an occasion for compassion toward the self and others, some become bitter and resentful. Wiesel shows that the suffering caused by the Holocaust, which certainly exceeded what human beings are normally asked to endure, evoked all these responses among the victims. He seems, however, most deeply troubled by the way in which suffering distorts a person. The protagonists of [Wiesel's book] *The Accident* insist that

> Suffering brings out the lowest, the most cowardly in man. There is a phase of suffering you reach beyond which you become a brute: beyond it you sell your soul—and worse, the souls of your friends—for a piece of bread, for some warmth, for a moment of oblivion, of sleep.

Those who undergo such suffering "no longer dare look at themselves in the mirror, afraid they may see their inner image: a monster. . . ."

For Elie Wiesel, victimization carried far enough and imposed brutally enough finally so distorts a person that he becomes unrecognizable even to himself. The victimization that occurred in the Holocaust revealed to Wiesel a capacity within the human soul that he could not have imagined during the days of his childhood in Sighet. An initial shock takes over Eliezer's soul when he sees that the Germans and his fellow Hungarians can be monstrous in their relationships to the Jews; a more unsettling disclosure is that God Himself can betray His people; but the final and perhaps most devastating shock arises from the disclosure that Eliezer himself is capable of disregard for his own father. The insight that no relationship is immune to the eruption of evil: this is what the experience of the Holocaust discloses to Wiesel.

Wiesel's Account of Genocide Forces His Readers to Become Witnesses

Lea Hamaoui

Lea Hamaoui is a Holocaust studies scholar and an associate professor of English at Kingsborough Community College in New York. Her works include a play on the Holocaust.

In the following selection, Lea Hamaoui proposes that Elie Wiesel's narrative describing the death camps purposely strips away the reader's defenses against knowing the true horror and degradation of the experience. As the townspeople of Sighet reject Moshe Beadle's warnings as unthinkable, readers are initially motivated to retain their illusions, even in the face of the reality of deportation and imprisonment, due to the dissonance between historical horror accounts and their known world. Going against the human impulse to reject such unthinkable experiences, Wiesel's descriptions force the reader to become a witness to the atrocities.

To render historical horror is to render, by definition, that which exceeds rendering; it projects pain for which there is no solace, no larger consolation, no redemptive possibility. The implications, both formal and aesthetic, for such a rendering are critical. The great tragedies negotiate exactly such a balance. . . . The young Eliezer staring into the mirror upon his liberation from Buchenwald [concentration camp] has also gained knowledge, but this knowledge in no way justifies the sufferings that preceeded it. It is not a sign of positive spiritual development. Nor is it linked to restorative changes in the moral and political realm. *Night* is not about a moral political order violated and restored, but about the shattering of the idea of such an order. . . .

Night proceeds from experience that is not universal. It does not expand from kernels of the familiar but from the unfamiliar, from data in historical reality. The deaths of Eliezer's father, of Akiva Drummer, of Juliek the violinist and of Meir Katz are different because, after all of the pain, there is nothing to be extracted by way of compensation. They are not symbolic but very real, and we experience, not a purging of feelings tapped but the fear of the unpredictable in life to which we, like the Jews of *Night*, are subject.

If symbol is something that stands in place of something else, the historical narrative does not stand in place of our experience, but alongside it. We experience historical narrative much the way we experience a neighbor's report of his or her visit to a place we have not ourselves visited. The report is informational—it is "adjacent" to our experience, neither interpretive nor metaphorical nor symbolic. It is "other" than our experience but also part of the same historical matrix within which we experience the flow of our own lives. *Night* threatens and disturbs in a way that symbolic narrative does not.

Night is Wiesel's attempt to bring word of the death camps back to humanity in such a form that his message, unlike that of Moshe the Beadle to Eliezer and to the Jews of Sighet, will not be rejected. The word I wish to stress here is *form*. The work, which is eyewitness account, is also much more than eyewitness account. In its rhetorical and aesthetic design, *Night* is shaped by the problematic of historical horror and by the resistances, both psychic and formal, to the knowledge Wiesel would convey.

When the narrator, Eliezer, sees a lorry filled with children who are dumped into a fiery ditch, he cannot believe what he has seen: "I pinched my face. Was I alive? Was I awake? I could not believe it. How could it be possible for them to

A view of some 150 bodies burned alive in a warehouse by the Nazis in order to prevent their liberation by American forces, 1945. William Vandivert/Time Life Pictures/Getty Images.

burn people, children, and for the world to keep silent? No, none of this could be true. It was a nightmare".

Eliezer cannot believe what is before his eyes. His disbelief seems to numb him physically—he pinches his face to ascertain that the medium of that vision, his body, is alive, perceiving, present. So fundamental is the horror to which he is an eyewitness that seeing comes at the expense of his bodily awareness of himself as a vital and perceiving entity. What Eliezer witnesses contradicts psychic underpinnings of existence so thoroughly that his very awareness brings with it feelings of deadness.

It is precisely this moment, this confrontation with data that negates the human impulses and ideas that structure our lives, with which Wiesel is concerned. We cannot know that which we cannot know. In order to bring the fact of Auschwitz [concentration camp] to us, Wiesel must deal with the inherent difficulty of assimilating the truth he would portray.

His method is simple, brilliant and depends upon a series of repetitions in which what is at stake is a breakdown of critical illusions. At this level, the experience of the reader reading the narrative is structurally parallel to his experience of life, at least as Karl Popper [a philosopher of science] describes it. Life, in Popper's view,

> resembles the experience of a blind person who runs into an obstacle and thereby experiences its existence. Through the falsification of our assumptions we actually make contact with "reality." The refutation of our errors is the positive experience we gain from reality.

Eliezer's tale is the story of a series of shattered expectations, his and our own. The repetition of this "disappointment," of optimism proven hollow and warnings rejected, becomes the crucial aesthetic fact or condition within which we then experience the narrator's account of his experiences in Auschwitz, in Buna, in Gleiwitz, and in Buchenwald. In this way we come to experience the account of the death camps as an account cleansed of past illusion, pristine in its terrible truth.

The quest for this truth is established at the outset of the narrative in the figure of Moshe the Beadle. Eliezer is devoted to his studies of Talmud. His decision to study Kabbalah with Moshe focuses the narrative on the problematic of reality and imbues it with the spiritual longings of this quest.

> There are a thousand and one gates leading into the orchard of mystical truth. Every human being has his own gate. . .

> And Moshe the Beadle, the poor barefoot of Sighet, talked to me for long hours of the revelations and mysteries of the

cabbala. It was with him that my initiation began. We would read together, ten times over, the same page of the Zohar. Not to learn it by heart, but to extract the divine essence from it.

And throughout those evenings a conviction grew in me that Moshe the Beadle would draw me with him into eternity, into that time where question and answer would become *one*.

The book, which begins with Eliezer's search for a teacher of mystical knowledge and ends with Eliezer's contemplating his image in a mirror after his liberation from Buchenwald, proposes a search for ultimate knowledge in terms that are traditional, while the knowledge it offers consists of data that is historical, radical, and subversive.

If directionality of the narrative is established early, a counter-direction makes itself felt very quickly. Following Eliezer's dream of a formal harmony, eternity and oneness toward which Moshe would take him, Eliezer's initiation into the "real" begins:

Then one day they expelled all the foreign Jews from Sighet. And Moshe the Beadle was a foreigner.

Crammed into cattle trains by Hungarian police, they wept bitterly. We stood on the platform and wept too.

Moshe is shot but escapes from a mass grave [the Ponar killing grounds] in one of the Galician forests of [Lithuania] near Kolomaye and returns to Sighet in order to warn the Jews there. He describes children used as targets for machine guns and the fate of a neighbor, Malka, and of Tobias the tailor.

From this point onward in the narrative, a powerful counter direction of flight away from truth, knowledge, reality, and history is set into motion. Moshe is not believed, not even by his disciple, Eliezer. The Jews of Sighet resist the news Moshe has brought them:

I wanted to come back to Sighet to tell you the story of my death . . . And see how it is, no one will listen to me. . .

And we, the Jews of Sighet, were waiting for better days, which would not be long in coming now.

Yes, we even doubted that he [German leader Adolf Hitler] wanted to exterminate us.

Was he going to wipe out a whole people? Could he exterminate a population scattered throughout so many countries? So many millions! What method could he use? And in the middle of the twentieth century?

Optimism persists with the arrival of the Germans. After Sighet is divided into a big and little ghetto, Wiesel writes, "little by little life returned to normal. The barbed wire which fenced us in did not cause us any real fear".

While the narrative presses simultaneously toward and away from the "real," the real events befalling the Jews of Sighet are perceived as unreal:

On everyone's back was a pack . . . Here came the Rabbi, his back bent, his face shaved, his pack on his back. His mere presence among the deportees added a touch of unreality to the scene. It was like a page torn from some story book, from some historical novel about the captivity of Babylon or the Spanish Inquisition.

The intensity of the resistance peaks in the boxcar in which Eliezer and his family are taken to the death camp. Madame Schächter, distraught by the separation from her pious husband and two older sons, has visions of fire: "Jews, listen to me! I can see a fire! There are huge flames! It is a furnace!" Her words prey on nerves, fan fears, dispel illusion: "We felt that an abyss was about to open beneath our bodies." She is gagged and beaten. As her cries are silenced the chimneys of Auschwitz come into view:

We had forgotten the existence of Madame Schächter. Suddenly we heard terrible screams: Jews, look! Look through the window! Flames! Look!

And as the train stopped, we saw this time that flames were gushing out of a tall chimney into the black sky.

The movement toward and away from the knowledge of historical horror that Moshe the Beadle brings back from the mass grave and the violence that erupts when precious illusions are disturbed, shapes the narrative of *Night*. The portrait and analysis of the resistances to knowing help situate the reader in relation to the historical narrative and imbue the narrative with the felt historicity of the world outside the book. Eliezer's rejection of the knowledge that Moshe brings back, literally, from the grave, predicts our own rejection of that knowledge. His failure to believe the witness prepares the reader for the reception of Eliezer's own story of his experience in Auschwitz by first examining the defenses that Eliezer, and, thereby, implicitly, the reader, would bring to descriptions of Auschwitz. The rejection of Moshe strips the reader of his own deafness in advance of the arrival at Auschwitz.

Once stripped of his defenses, the reader moves from a fortified, to an open, undefended position vis-à-vis the impact of the narrative. Because the lines between narrative art and life have been erased, Wiesel brings the reader into an existential relationship to the historical experience recounted in *Night*. By virtue of that relationship, the reader is transformed into a witness. The act of witnessing is ongoing for most of the narrative, a narrative that is rife with horror and with the formal dissonances that historically experienced horror must inflict upon language.

Human extremity challenges all formal representation of it. It brings the world of language and the world outside language into the uncomfortable position of two adjacent notes on a piano keyboard that are simultaneously pressed and held. The sounds they produce jar the ear. In a work of historical horror, language and life, expression and experience are perceived as separate opaque structures, each of which is inadequate to encompass the abyss that separates them.

The most powerful passages in *Night* are those that mark Eliezer's arrival in Auschwitz. The family is separated. Eliezer and his father go through a selection and manage to stay together. Eliezer watches a truck drop living children into a ditch full of flames. He and his father conclude that this is to be Eliezer's fate as well. Eliezer decides he will run into an electrified wire fence and electrocute himself rather than face an excruciating death in the flaming ditch.

The moment is extraordinary and extreme beyond the wildest of human imaginings. Hearing his fellow Jews murmur the Kaddish, a formula of praise of the Almighty that is the traditional prayer for the dead, Eliezer revolts: "For the first time, I felt revolt rise up in me. Why should I bless His name? The Eternal Lord of the Universe, the All-Powerful and Terrible, was silent. What had I to thank Him for?" The Jews continue their march and Eliezer begins to count the steps before he will jump at the wire:

> Ten steps still. Eight. Seven. We marched slowly on, as though following a hearse at our own funeral . . . There it was now, right in front of us, the pit and its flames. I gathered all that was left of my strength, so that I could break from the ranks and throw myself upon the barbed wire. In the depths of my heart, I bade farewell to my father, to the whole universe.

And the words of the Kaddish, hallowed by centuries and disavowed only moments before, words of praise and of affirmation of divine oneness, spring unbidden to his lips: "and in spite of myself, the words formed themselves and issued in a whisper from my lips: *Yitgadal veyitkadach shme raba* . . . May His name be blessed and magnified". Eliezer does not run to the wire. The entire group turns left and enters a barracks. . . ."

The words of the Kaddish in *Night* do not express the horror to which Eliezer is a witness. They flow from an inner necessity and do not reflect but deflect that horror. They project the sacredness of life in the face of its most wrenching desecration. They affirm life at the necessary price of disaffirming the surrounding reality. The world of experience and the world of language could not, at this moment, be further apart. Experience is entirely beyond words. Words are utterly inadequate to convey experience.

Societal Breakdown During Transit and Deportation of Holocaust Victims

Simone Gigliotti

Simone Gigliotti is a senior lecturer at Victoria University of Wellington in New Zealand. She is also a member of the executive committee of the International Network of Genocide Scholars and has published extensively on the Holocaust.

The deportation and transportation experience of the Jews in the Holocaust represents, in Simone Gigliotti's view, a microcosm of social collapse. The degrading and humiliating conditions, and the cruel, deliberate processing by the captors, served to strip the deportees of their dignity by physically and psychologically overwhelming their senses. The Nazis' choice of cattle cars for most transport reflected their view of the victims as subhuman. All sense of time and certainty was replaced by lack of privacy, terror, and abandonment. As a result, the victims' own social conventions and proprieties were eroded. In the following excerpt, Gigliotti states that the inhuman conditions demonstrate that the Nazis were less concerned with relocation than extermination and that the victims did not make the relocation journey willingly.

From October 1941 until the end of 1944, an estimated three million Jews were transported from major ghettos to their deaths by trains under the orders of [German leader Adolf] Hitler and the Nazi regime. The inhumane, claustro-

Simone Gigliotti, *Approaches to Teaching Wiesel's Night*, New York: The Modern Language Association of America, 2007. Copyright © 2007 by the Modern Language Association of America. Reproduced by permission of the Modern Language Association of America.

phobic, and debilitating conditions deportees experienced in the train journeys are some of the last and most illuminating untold episodes of captivity and displacement in the Holocaust. . . .

This essay considers . . . the space of traumatic transit, largely detoured by historians, by examining Wiesel's Holocaust memoir *Night*. What does *Night* reveal about the deportation experience that historians writing about the Holocaust cannot? In what ways does the journey represent a microcosm of social collapse? How does Wiesel's representation of transit add to the teaching of the history of deportations?

Historians have, overwhelmingly, represented Nazi deportation policy in ways that confirm a stereotype of an efficient bureaucracy employed in the business of mass murder. Using mainly perpetrator documents, historians have reconstructed a procedure for deportations that identified the logistical determinants and financing of transports across Europe; the contribution of national railways from Germany and occupied Greece, Poland, and France; and the administrative and legal complexities that classified a person as "deportable." Despite their important contribution, these approaches echo the perpetrators' view of their victims as objects of a process. They leave the reader at the station platform as the trains depart, outside the deportees' traumatic confinement. The narrative journey of deportation resumes on the platforms of arrival at the concentration camps.

Before investigating *Night* and its themes, it is necessary to provide a context for the function of deportations in the development of the final solution. The decision-making process and the emergence of Hitler's order for the final solution are topics of ongoing debate among historians. By adopting this contextual approach, instructors can introduce a larger historical narrative in which to place *Night*.

Victims' Accounts of Deportation Illustrate Trauma

How can historians' narratives of deportation as a process and victims' interpretation of it intersect? [Holocaust scholar] Raul Hilberg and [history professor] Alfred C. Mierzejewski emphasize the logistical features of deportation, such as scheduling Jews on *Sonderzüge* ("special trains") to fit within existing timetables, the application of concession fares to transports of four hundred or more Jews, free travel for children under four, Jewish self-financing of the one-way journeys with expropriated property, and the coordination of the SS and the *Deutsche Reichsbahn* (German Railways) to implement it. Their analyses provide a critical foundation for interpreting Nazi approaches and contradictions: the use of boxcars and cattle cars for most deportations was evidence of the perpetrators' view of their victims as subhuman and continued the dehumanization that was a central theme of Nazi antisemitic ideology. Transportation to "the East" was presented to victims as relocation (there were provisions of food and clothing and luggage requirements) and as a means of survival, so as to encourage deportees' compliance and agreement in boarding the train. If this was a faithful representation, then why inflict such intolerable conditions as spatial compression, climactic assault, and humiliation of the victims? These conditions conspired to overwhelm them physically and psychologically and made their preparedness for alleged labor in "the East" all the more unlikely.

The deportees' anticipation of work, however, depended on the believability of rumours and the knowledge of what was happening to those Jews who were forcibly resettled, and this information varied greatly in select occupied areas and ghettos. At the time of Wiesel's deportation with his family, in the spring of 1944, news of gassings of Jews at Treblinka [concentration camp in Poland], which had been occurring since the summer of 1942, and the connotation of a trip to "the

East" as a journey of no return were still largely unknown among Sighet's prospective deportees. Instructors thus need to situate Wiesel's narrative of life in Sighet, in northern Transylvania, Romania: the region's annexation by Hungary in 1940, the Nazi occupation of Hungary in late March 1944, and finally the ghettoization of Sighet's Jews. This coverage of the historical background can condition students, in the very least, to the context of the uncertainty, isolation, and incarceration faced by Jewish communities in many small towns like Wiesel's and to the departure scene in *Night*: "The synagogue resembled a large railroad station: baggage and tears".

Wiesel's testimony of deportation transports the reader into a physical and historically distinct space of trauma that resists easy interpretation. His account of the conditions of transit—the compression of bodies, the separation of families, the lack of material provisions, the terror of temporal uncertainty, and the profound abandonment represented by the isolation of human beings in a cattle car en route to death—has been corroborated in countless other testimonies. Of course, there was no typical deportation experience, as individual narrative, context, time of deportation, duration of journey, number of people in each car, and other factors determined each victim's response.

Deportation Narrative Eliminates Abstract View

And yet despite the journey's narrative and historical function—providing a passage from one form of incarceration to something altogether unimaginable—these transit experiences have been largely seen in abstraction, too traumatic, emotional, and subjective to be of important historical use. On entering the space of the cattle car, readers become suspended travelers and invasive witnesses to unspeakable trauma and the degradation of human beings. What can testimonies of this experience—so singular, extreme, and disturbing—do for historical approaches to the Holocaust? I argue that testimonies of deportation destabilize cognitive control of historical representation as a factually legitimated, ordered, and chronologically constructed event. Instructors might use these testimonies to investigate this destabilization of factual control, in addition to the erasure of trauma in historical representation; the role of emotion in narrative history; and the adoption of a sensory paradigm, as offered by the physiological response to the train journey, in interpretations of witnessing.

Mobility and immobility were constant companions of Wiesel's even before his involuntary departure from Sighet. In the synagogue, where Wiesel and others were awaiting deportation, the scene was desperate and chaotic. The next day, when they were marched to the station, the Hungarian police forced them into the cattle car. Wiesel described the experience thus:

> [E]ighty persons in each one. They handed us some bread, a few pails of water. They checked the bars on the windows to make sure they would not come loose. The cars were sealed. One person was placed in charge of every car: if someone managed to escape, that person would be shot.

Wiesel paints an image of imprisonment—bars, limited vision, and surveillance. Historians might contest his count of eighty people in the cattle car on the grounds that numbers vary substantially among survivors' accounts. His estimate would require some documentation from SS records about the number of people in that transport. Whether or not the exact number of people can be verified, as Wiesel does not say how that number was arrived at, does not negate the impression of suffocation, the feeling of intense overcrowding, and the destruction of intimacy and personal boundaries, conditions common in many deportees' accounts.

Wiesel's Deportation Journey

Wiesel's account of the deportation offers a rare type of witnessing. Owing to the hermetic architecture and overwhelming darkness of the cattle car, the narrator's memory of what happened during the journey seemed less influenced by what he saw than by what his other senses told him, and his witnessing became an embodied act that displaced the reliance on vision. In embodied witnessing, what one feels, smells, hears, and cannot see constantly threaten one's sanity, faith, and any hope for normality, however defiantly construed. (This effect is especially evident in Wiesel's representation of Mrs. Schächter.) The heat from bodily compression and the thirst from lack of water produced desperation and tension, as well as a loosening of the bondage to accepted convention.

Spatial compression in deportation journeys was prefaced with overcrowding in ghettos, although the threat to practicing civility and the performance of private acts in public was not as common. Whatever remained in the ghetto of an individual's or family's physical belongings and identity was further expropriated for the deportation journey, since deportees were only permitted to take a specified weight of luggage and clothes. These material expropriations were incomparable, however, to the subversion of conventional behavior, practice, and response and the effect of this subversion on individual and communal adjustment to the journey, including the victims' management of some irritating deportees. Wiesel's journey became a time of release of inhibitions and erotic feeling, the darkness of night acting as an anonymous stimulant:

> Freed of normal constraints, some of the young let go of their inhibitions and, under cover of darkness, caressed one another, without any thought of others, alone in the world. The others pretended not to notice.

The uncertainty of the train's destination produced a need for the preservation of food and water, and the labor of surveillance and preventing escape was transferred from the German guards to the deportees themselves. This mode of management and control aimed to instill intense fear and terror in the deportees during the journey. Attempts at escape were punished through violence against the majority.

Time and Chronology Not Definable

Although Wiesel's representation of the cattle car journey is not unlike many others at this point, the historian might be nervous about the lack of reference to time and chronology in *Night*. When was Wiesel moved into the ghetto? When was he deported and with whom? How many days did the journey take? But arguably such questions, evidence of a need to ground these events in wartime reality, do not bring us much closer to interpreting the historical utility of Wiesel's journey. While such questions should be answered, they are not the only pertinent questions. What questions, then, can be asked of the relation between chronology and intensifying trauma, between time and testimony? How does the train journey escape historical time and destabilize cognitive control?

It is in the journey where time and chronology are no longer defined by quantifiable units but, in Wiesel's memory, by traumatic events that punctuate time's passage from day to night. One of the more unsettling episodes occurs in the uncontrolled and periodically terrifying screams of Mrs. Schächter, a woman who was traveling with her ten-year-old son and whose husband and two elder sons were inadvertently deported previously without her. She yelled, "Fire! I see a fire! I see a fire!" as she looked out through the barred windows of the cattle car. Her screams are shocking, not only because of what fire has come to symbolize from a postwar perspective but also because the deportees could see "[o]nly the darkness of night". Wiesel reports her continuing visions, as though her descent into delusion was marked by increasingly vivid and animated scenes of fire. Her screams created a collective trauma in the wagon:

> Our terror could no longer be contained. Our nerves had reached a breaking point. Our very skin was aching. It was as though madness had infected all of us. We gave up. A few young men forced her to sit down, then bound and gagged her.

Here Wiesel narrates how, during the temporary muting of Mrs. Schächter's screams, the train's rhythmic movement added an air of welcome routine to the journey. Yet her insistent cries soon intensified, finally culminating in "Look at the fire! Look at the flames! Flames everywhere . . .". The physical violence that silenced her screaming, as Wiesel tells it, became accepted in the carriage, not because violence was an acceptable practice but because, in the space of the cattle car, a degree of toleration and management had to be imposed for the mental preservation of the majority. The ferocity of the men's blows was a reflection of deportees' repression of their possible fate, for she was a reminder of what they feared—surrender to delirium and incomprehension.

Mrs. Schächter finally paused in her outbursts, but again her muteness was only temporary. The darkness of night, as I interpret from Wiesel's figurative and literal use of it, was the catalyst for an uninhibited truth too painful to comprehend and the canvas on which the flames yet again saturated her vision:

> Toward evening she began to shout again:
>
> "The fire, over there!"
>
> She was pointing somewhere in the distance, always the same place. No one felt like beating her anymore. The heat, the thirst, the stench, the lack of air, were suffocating us. Yet

all that was nothing compared to her screams, which tore us apart. A few more days and all of us would have started to scream.

As the train arrived at Auschwitz [concentration camp], Mrs. Schächter's vision was confirmed:

And as the train stopped, this time we saw flames rising from a tall chimney into a black sky.

Mrs. Schächter had fallen silent on her own. Mute again, indifferent, absent, she had returned to her corner.

Historians' Accounts Cannot Equal Victims' Story of Terror

Wiesel's narration of Mrs. Schächter's public outbursts of her private torment—predictions, when read retrospectively—carries the reader into a space not accessible from reading historians' accounts of deportation. The illumination of the journey's assault on the senses, such as the piercing volume of Mrs. Schächter's screams, renders this experience as one of continuous reliving, a psychologically relentless transit moment of no escape. The moment occurred in historical time, as a part of Wiesel's narrative, but also outside it, in "traumatic time"; the journey experience is disjointed and highlights the psychological descent and terror of the victims, as well as their complete abandonment.

The themes in Wiesel's narrative common to other victims' accounts—the eradication of privacy, the erosion of intimacy, the relaxation of social convention regulating erotic and violent behavior, the humiliation of using the pail to defecate or urinate, and the communal spatial exchange for sleeping and standing that developed among deportees—explode the bureaucratic presentation of deportation as relocation, a journey to a work camp. It is the deportation journey that functions as the stripping or shedding stage of the self from the past, from social convention and expectations of improvement and promise. The physical and psychological endurance of the days of travel undo, essentially, one's ability to retain resolve, moral strength, and purpose. If the deportees were under the impression that they were meant to survive the trip, instructors may also use the deportations as evidence of a major corrective to the controversial perception of deportees as ostensibly voluntary, willing, and docile victims. Instructors can reflect on the deception of the Nazi image of relocation that characterized deportation journeys and the undoing of that image: the deplorable conditions of transit, the number of deportees crammed into each car, and the almost immediate killing of women and children, the sick and the elderly who arrived at the camps. The differences in the types of carriages used—passenger cars for Jews from Western Europe and cattle cars for Jews in the *Generalgouvernement* and more distant regions such as Greece—reinforced the Nazi perception of civilized, assimilated Jewry in the West and so-called primitive Jewry in the East. While the method of transport was not always consistent, these distinctions reflected the pretense of travel in those areas where resistance may have been encountered.

When used with other testimonies of deportation, survivor narratives can further corroborate and legitimate what historians have represented as a well-rehearsed process of identification, extraction from the community, and transportation. Deportation was an administrative and detached process that involved the Jewish councils, acting on Nazi instruction to compile deportation lists; the Jewish police, assisting in roundups; and, finally, the use of railways, which required the aid of auxiliary officers who guarded deportation trains and railway workers who patrolled the stations. In addition to causing us to rethink the realm of ordinary workers and antisemitic perpetrators involved in this task, the testimonies give a voice and identity not only to those victims who survived but also to those who, in [Holocaust survivor] Primo Levi's words, "drowned" and are obscured in the anonymity of the magnitude of six million deaths.

God's Failure to Prevent Genocide Presents an Absurd Universe

Josephine Knopp

Josephine Knopp is an instructor in the English department at Broward College in Fort Lauderdale, Florida.

The traditional Jewish view of life's meaning is derived from the Torah, which is a manifestation of God, states Josephine Knopp in the following selection. The Jews' covenant with God is one of equal protection: God assumes responsibility for the Jews, and they protect the Torah. However, the reality of Auschwitz concentration camp and the Holocaust call this alliance into question, says Knopp. Since God is "in control" of actual history, the Jews have no choice but to connect God with their suffering at the hands of the Nazis. Acknowledging that the covenant with God is no longer valid would shake the very foundations of Judaism. Faced with an absurd religious and moral dilemma, Elie Wiesel and other victims were forced to protest against God and demand he fulfill his responsibilities under the covenant.

Elie Wiesel, journalist and novelist of the Holocaust, claims to owe his writing career to three years of imprisonment in Nazi concentration camps, starting at the age of fourteen. He relates in his quasi-autobiographical works that in the Hungarian *shtetl* of his early years he had been completely immersed in Talmudic studies (in the time-honored manner of intelligent Jewish boys), presumably preparing for life as a Talmudic scholar. His world was that of orthodox Judaism, governed in every detail by Jewish law, outside the mainstream of European culture.

Josephine Knopp, "Wiesel and the Absurd," *Contemporary Literature*, vol. 15, Spring 1974, pp. 212–220. Copyright © 1974 by the Board of Regents of the University of Wisconsin System. Reproduced by permission.

A rabbi of the Romanian Jewish community reads a prayer at the Great Synagogue during a 2009 commemoration in Bucharest, Romania, for those killed in a revolt led by members of the Iron Guard fascist party in 1941. About 800,000 Jews lived in Romania before World War II; half of them died during the war or were sent to concentration camps. AP Images.

To the young Wiesel the notion of an "absurd" universe would have been a completely alien one. Indeed, the world of orthodox Judaism would appear to allow no place in it for notions of the absurd in the contemporary, existential sense. For the traditional Jewish view holds that life's structure and meaning are fully explained and indeed derive from the divinely granted Torah. Yet, this view of Judaism, while accurate on the most basic level, is simplistic, ignoring, as it does, the well-established Jewish tradition of challenging God by questioning His ways. While Job is the most obvious (and perhaps the best) example to cite in this connection, it should not be forgotten that other prominent figures of the Old Testament, including Abraham, Moses, and Jeremiah, rebel against God and hold Him responsible for the injustice of the world.

As witness to the Holocaust, Elie Wiesel, remaining firmly within this Judaic tradition of protest, cries out against the destruction of European Jewry, against God's failure to intercede on behalf of His creatures. Wiesel's first five novels, in fact, can be meaningfully read as a sustained, developing revolt against God from within a Jewish context. Jewish tradition provides not only adequate precedents for such revolt, but the legal and moral sanction as well, in the unique covenant with God into which the Jewish people entered: "We are to protect His Torah, and He, in turn, assumes responsibility for Israel's presence in the world. Thus, when our spirituality—the Torah—was in danger, we used force in protecting it; but when our physical existence was threatened, we simply reminded God of His duties and promises deriving from the covenant." In effect, the covenant brings God and man into a moral partnership, with each of the two parties having a clearly defined responsibility to the other.

Against this background the reality of Auschwitz confronts the Jew with a dilemma, an "absurdity" which cannot be dismissed easily and which stubbornly refuses to dissipate of its own accord. "In faithfulness to Judaism . . . [the] Jew must refuse to disconnect God from the holocaust." Since the Jewish God is "a God who is Lord of actual history, its external events included," it is an inescapable conclusion that "Auschwitz is not an accident . . . because of the fact that God is part of it." Thus, the continued validity of the covenant itself is called into serious question. Clearly, any recognition that the covenant might no longer be operative would strike a devastating blow at the very foundations of Judaism and leave the theologically serious Jew isolated, to struggle in an unaccustomed loneliness with an indifferent, or worse, hostile universe. After Auschwitz, he is joined to the French existentialists in being confronted with the absurdity of the universe, an absurdity engendered and given substance by the Holocaust and signaling the breakdown of the covenant. The only possible response that remains within the framework of Judaism is denunciation of God and a demand that He fulfill His contractual obligation.

This is the religious and moral context within which Wiesel attempts to apprehend and assimilate the events of the Holocaust. It would appear to be an underlying purpose of Wiesel's creative efforts to reconcile Auschwitz with Judaism, to confront and perhaps wring meaning from the absurd, which emerges as the true antagonist in his fiction. In this respect Wiesel is on common ground with other Jewish writers of the Holocaust, notably André Schwarz-Bart and Nelly Sachs, whose poetry, according to her own description, is "always intent upon raising the unspeakable to a transcendental plane, in order to make it tolerable.". . .

[Like French writer Albert Camus] Wiesel has seriously considered [suicide] in his novel, *The Accident*, whose protagonist-narrator is almost killed in an "accident" that is an apparent attempt at suicide. With this act Wiesel's rebellion against the God of Judaism, begun passionately in the setting of Nazi concentration camps in the autobiographical *Night* and continued on a more detached, philosophical plane in his second novel, *Dawn*, reaches a climax. For the sacredness of life, as God's gift to mankind, is basic to Judaism and in fact arguably the most basic tenet of the Jewish faith. In the Jewish view it is not for man to judge "whether life is or is not worth living"; only the God of Israel, as Creator and Giver of Life, is to determine when life is to end. In Wiesel's peculiarly Jewish context, therefore, the suicide attempt takes on added significance as a kind of ultimate defiance of God, explainable only on the basis of a recognition, in reaction to Auschwitz, that God encompasses evil as well as good, that in violating His covenant with man, God has not only withdrawn His protection but has left man free of the restraints of His laws and commandments. . . .

Wiesel's character is obsessed by the relationship of man and God. It is of great significance that although Eliezer, the young protagonist of *Night*, bitterly and repeatedly denounces God, "who chose us from among the races to be tortured day and night," he remains a Jew and never loses his belief in God's presence in the world: "I did not deny God's existence, but I doubted His absolute justice". . . .

Suicide is not the answer for Wiesel, who finds his solution instead in protest, not merely against absurdity, but against God Himself. The nature of this protest has been described by Wiesel: "The Jew, in my view, may rise against God, provided he remains within God. One can be a very good Jew, observe all the *Mitzvot*, study Talmud—and yet be against God". The apparent contradiction in Wiesel's position is in fact explainable on the basis of the covenant. For him the object of protest against God is not nihilism, not denial of God, but the very opposite—the re-establishment of God's order in a world which has witnessed the destruction of order. Indeed, through Michael [the protagonist in Wiesel's *The Gates of the Forest*], Wiesel confesses his inability to repudiate God: "I want to blaspheme, and I can't quite manage it. I go up against Him, I shake my fist, I froth with rage, but it's still a way of telling Him that He's there, that He exists . . . that denial itself is an offering to His grandeur".

Though Wiesel clings to God in the face of injustice, his position cannot be termed philosophical suicide, in the sense in which Camus understands that phrase. On the contrary, Wiesel is a perfect example of Camus' "absurd man," striving for clarity whatever the consequences, recognizing the complicity of God in the evil perpetrated by man, in spite of the shattering effect of such recognition: "The student of the Talmud, the child that I was, had been consumed in the flames". For Wiesel, thus, there is no "leap of faith" but rather what may be termed a leap *away* from faith, although it is not successfully realized. The boy of *Night*, who vows never to "forget those flames which consumed my faith forever," gives way to the man of *Gates of the Forest*, who understands that "God's final victory . . . lies in man's inability to reject Him" and has "only one purpose: not to cause others to suffer".

Meaningful Silences in *Night* Convey the Unspeakable

Jack Kolbert

Jack Kolbert was a professor of modern and classical languages. Kolbert, who died in 2005, met Elie Wiesel while at the University of New Mexico. As a result of that friendship, Kolbert wrote The Worlds of Elie Wiesel: An Overview of His Career and His Major Themes. *Kolbert authored ten books, as well as essays on French culture and related topics.*

In the following excerpt, Jack Kolbert states that, in spite of his skill as a writer, Elie Wiesel found language inadequate to describe the horrors of life in the concentration camps. The Holocaust was so irrational and unthinkable that words had not been created to fully illuminate the experience. In spite of these challenges, Wiesel did not want the innocent victims' lives and stories to disappear without recognition. To overcome this obstacle, observes Kolbert, Night *is written in carefully chosen prose juxtaposed with meaningful silences that convey more than words are capable of describing. The use of minimalist language requires that each word carry great meaning. Silences are prompts for the reader's imagination to fill in the void.*

Elie Wiesel is much more than a fulltime writer: he teaches, lectures, counsels major world leaders. For many years he was also a journalist. Above all, however, he is a writer! In all of his work, he depends upon words, sentences, paragraphs. Language is his tool of the trade. He writes in French, Hebrew, Yiddish, English. He can also function somewhat in German and Hungarian. In whatever language he selects to write, words become the soul of his métier [profession]. If words serve as the tools that make his works possible, they often become—paradoxically—major impediments or barriers to his art of communication. While Wiesel the writer/speaker/ teacher/journalist cannot function without words, these same words become painful, tyrannical hindrances that constrict and constrain.

Holocaust Defies Description

In Wiesel's creative activities, one discerns a pendulum oscillating between his desire to express his thought and experiences, on one hand, and his personal frustration at not being able adequately to transmit those same thoughts and experiences on the other hand. His career has been replete with awesome frays between words and non-words (or silences): "Words separate me from myself . . . In searching for silence, in digging into it, I started to discover the perils and the powers of the spoken word . . . Words seem stale, foolish, inadequate, artificial, anemic; I wanted them to be fiery . . . The language of night was not human but animalistic, even mineral-like: raucous cries, howling, muffled sighs, savage complaints, blows of the cudgel [a short, heavy club]."

What does a writer do when he is overpowered by the irrepressible urge to communicate a verbal message, but his words do not have the power to express what he wishes to say? The events of the Holocaust, the pain felt by Wiesel, the grief suffered by him at the loss of his family and closest friends—these are the traumatic experiences that often transcend linguistic description. He once told [journalist] Brigitte-Fanny Cohen that "I know that words do not have the power of transmitting the message that I carry inside of me, nor even a fragment of the message. In vain do I try to say the unsayable in order to express my impossibility of saying [these things]. If I succeed in convincing a reader or an auditor that we cannot communicate this experience, I would not have spoken in vain." Wiesel thus believes that his mission as a writer/speaker has been achieved even if what he says is not the whole truth, but at least it conveys a reasonably accurate shadow of the truth. In the unique case of the Holocaust, the whole truth can never really be retrieved by the witness to an auditor or reader who was not present at the scene of the event. However, even a portion of the truth is preferable to total silence.

Wiesel Uses Words and Silence to Convey Horrors

In effect, the texts of Elie Wiesel, both written and spoken, consist of an ingenious interplay between words and silence. That a professional writer should reveal his lack of faith in the power and magic of language is an uncommon phenomenon. After all, what other tools are available to the writer? It is even more unusual for a devout Jew like Wiesel to suspect the efficacy of language. Jews have traditionally enjoyed, deservedly, the reputation of being the people of the Book. The central tenets of Jewish faith emerge out of their reading and analyses of the Torah, a sacred work constructed of words, sentences, syntax, accent marks—in short, all of the accoutrements [trappings or equipment] of language. How could such a deeply religious man like Wiesel doubt the potential of language? His skepticism about language alternates with his celebration of language. His ambivalence on the subject is reflected by the way he combines a judicious suppression of words with an equally judicious enthusiasm for words. Through his painstaking manipulation of utterances and taciturnity he has somehow managed to construct the texts that he eagerly transmits to his readers.

Wiesel does not idolize language for the sake of language. He does not consider language to be an end in itself. Rather, for him, language is merely a tool, a literary aid. It possesses the power of uniting people and also of dividing them into sects and cults. Wiesel, for his part, chooses to utilize language as a dynamic force that brings people together. While language can be used both to clarify issues and to cloud them, he prefers to use his texts to elucidate and clarify issues, not to obscure them.

The issue of language—how it functions in the process of communication between an author and his public—this issue has always been a key element in how Wiesel views literature. This is so possibly because he opted to write in an adopted language, French, rather than in one of his mother tongues. This explains in part his fascination with Samuel Beckett, the Irish writer who also preferred to write in an acquired language, French, instead of in English or Irish. Wiesel also admired Beckett because "The impossibility of human communication is, by the way, the main theme of all of his work." (This is of course also true of Wiesel's works.)

The consideration of the role of language in literary creativity occupies an important place in Wiesel's thinking. In fact, the conflict between words and silence has always been a traumatic obsession for him. We can identify at least three major elements that explain this conflict. First, Wiesel seems governed by what the French call *pudeur*, a reticence to speak too freely about people's private lives. This *pudeur* is certainly apparent in his discussions of his own personal life. An almost untranslatable term, *pudeur* suggests the idea of reserve, modesty, the need to conceal one's emotions. . . .

Wiesel Uses Minimal Language for Greatest Impact

The second element in Wiesel's silence is his basic philosophy of life, a philosophy in which he stresses that the finest literary texts are those in which the densest, the most complex subject matter ought to be stated in the smallest possible number of words. Wiesel must then be regarded as a minimalist, one who seeks to convey his message by limiting himself to the unavoidable essentials, and nothing more. At all costs, his ideas must be stated with few frills and sparse verbal ornamentation. Consciously he chooses to express his thoughts in simple, clear, uncomplicated, and straightforward language. The extraneous details have been eliminated. Each word must have a purpose. And each word must be chosen so that it is as pregnant with meaning as possible. In this respect, Wiesel's literary art is consistent with the finest traditions of French classicism, a movement for which he had much admiration.

That Wiesel waited ten years [after his liberation from the concentration camps] before he plunged into his literary career corroborates both his fascination with the use of language and his fear of resorting to it. During this ten-year gestation he waged his battle between words and silence. . . . Eventually the desire to tell his story became irrepressible. In [his book] *Signes d'exode* Wiesel admits his difficulty in "describing the indescribable." At a rare moment of candor he confesses his fear of language: "I felt I needed ten years to collect words and the silence in them. . . . I am obsessed with silence because I am afraid of the spoken word, even of the written word."

Moments of Silence Convey Emotions

How to depict verbally the horror of the concentration camps? This was the central challenge facing the writer as he prepared to enter the realm of literature. He knew that he would have to overcome not only the inadequacy of vocabulary, but also the awesome task of interspersing language with the appropriate use of silence. Even grammatical construction raised many barriers. The events of the Shoah [the Holocaust] were so illogical, so irrational that they did not readily conform to the established contours of syntactic logic. As Wiesel composed his sentences, he posed many questions; for example: "Can you even communicate Auschwitz by structuring it in literary form?" In the end, however, he learned that by deftly alternating meaningful moments of silence with well-chosen language, he could vanquish the obstacles arising out of the grammatical constraints.

In his novels Wiesel likes to interrupt the flow of spoken dialogue between his characters by inserting into their speech pregnant pauses of silence, leaving it up to the reader's imagination to fill in the voids between the words. In *Night*, for example, as a mother passes in front of suffering children in the concentration camp, she becomes mute and even turns her eyes away from them, pretending to ignore their pain by distancing herself physically and physiologically from their wailing and their pain. Without uttering a single word, her gestures and taciturnity suggest to the reader the intense agony she obviously feels at the plight of these children. . . . Wiesel seems to imply that words can often mask the truth, whereas silence speaks with eloquence. In the major Wieselean novels, whenever the characters suffer intensely, their pain is transmitted to us much more effectively through silence than through speech. Wiesel has written that "Silence does not always signify absence of speech; it signifies also presence beyond speech."

In some of Wiesel's other novels some of the most fascinating fictional personalities are those who have lost their speech, who have become either totally or partially mute. Their tongues have been frozen by their recollections of the brutal experiences they witnessed in the Holocaust. Even God, traumatized by the atrocities committed by the human beings He had created, has been rendered speechless. The silence of God, the inability of God to play an active role by expressing His outrage, that silence and that inability to act are both major themes in Wieselean texts. If for many of the survivors of Treblinka and Auschwitz, God has died, for Wiesel, at least, his God remains very much alive; but He has become inexplicably speechless and paralyzed by the shock of witnessing human evil.

Silence need not at all be considered as an enemy of literature. When managed skillfully by a writer, it can, ironically, be
seen as a potent tool that enhances the writer's ability to communicate a compelling message. In literary works, one encounters all kinds of silences—those that drown out speech
entirely and those that enrich it. Wiesel's silence is the kind
that enriches language. Once he wrote as follows: "Of course,
my silence is meant to be a very eloquent silence, a shouting
silence."

Following his famous ten-year wait, Wiesel made a conscious decision to bring silence to a halt. He knew that unless
he ended his muteness and resorted to language, the Shoah
would gradually evaporate into the mist of passing history. He
realized that his testimony needed to be recorded; otherwise it
would disappear with his own death someday. In the name of
the six million he became the instrument that would keep
their memory alive. It thus fell upon Wiesel's shoulders to assume the responsibility for reminding the world for all time
to come that the Holocaust had destroyed millions of lives, a
rich cultural heritage, and almost an entire civilization. For
the author of *Night* it became a sacred duty to fill the universe
with the haunting memory of those who had been destroyed.
If the lives of these innocent victims had been demolished, at
least Wiesel's books would guarantee that the story of their
destruction would remain forever.

Wiesel Creates Mystical Fusion of Language and Silence

There is something mystical or spiritual about Elie Wiesel's
fusion of language and silence. This mystical, spiritual quality
even lends to his prose a certain poetic quality. In fact, one
might say that Wiesel's prose combines poetry, prayer, chant-
ing, and many quiet moments that are interspersed between
the uttered words. For the highly regarded twentieth-century
French critic, Abbé Bremond, prayer emerges out of poetry; in

fact, the two were almost consubstantial [having the same substance]. For Elie Wiesel too, there is an inextricably close relationship between the two. As he chanted the Kaddish and the Yizkor, those well-known Jewish prayers for the dead, he recited the poetry of memory honoring the deceased. This kind of poetic prayer has always been a central part of the Hebrew religious service. Remarkable also in this service is the vital interplay between spoken or chanted prayer, on the one hand, and solemn silence (referred to as the Amidah in the Jewish prayer book), on the other. As in the Jewish prayer service, one finds in the literary endeavors of Elie Wiesel an impressive harmony between poetic language and eloquent silence. This harmony between the spoken and the unspoken forms the core of Wiesel's oeuvre. Here is how he came close to defining his own entire body of literature: "When a thousand words are pressed into a single line, a poem is born. In Literature the weight of silence determines the weight of art."

Wiesel's Memoir Is a Testament to Recovery from the Holocaust

David Patterson

David Patterson is director of Bornblum Judaic Studies Program at the University of Memphis (Tennessee). He has taught numerous courses on topics including Israel, Jewish thought, and the Holocaust.

In the following selection, David Patterson states that in the act of writing his memoir, Elie Wiesel provides testament to the act of recovering the value and meaning of life. Night *is Wiesel's testimony against the indifference of humanity. By demonstrating care and concern for others, Wiesel is negating the Nazis' campaign to destroy those values. Further, says Patterson, the Jews' belief in the holiness of every human being sustained survivors such as Wiesel. Indeed, their God could not have died if they and their humanity have survived.*

Coming to the end of *Night*, Wiesel comes to no end. It is as though he remains inside the sealed train and, like Mrs. Schächter, is shouting to us, "Jews, listen to me, . . . I see a fire! I see flames, huge flames!" And yet this very shouting, this very testimony, might open up a path back to life. And the fact that we hold Wiesel's memoir in our hands means that there is something of value to be understood in this testimony, some matter of great urgency that must be transmitted.

What, then, might be gathered from Wiesel's choice to endure the ordeal of putting to paper the memory of this radical

David Patterson, *Approaches to Teaching Wiesel's* Night, New York: The Modern Language Association of America, 2007. Copyright © 2007 by the Modern Language Association of America. Reproduced by permission of the Modern Language Association of America.

assault on his very soul? In this memoir, as in other Holocaust memoirs, recovery is the key to this question. And the word *recovery* is to be understood on at least two levels:

> The recovery of value and meaning in life through the testimony to its undoing. For Wiesel, this recovery entails some sort of recovery of the sacred teachings of the Jewish tradition.

> A recovery in the sense of recovering from the illness of a deaf and indifferent humanity that, through its indifference, lost its humanity. There is also a certain indifference that overcomes those who were abandoned by humanity.

These aspects of recovery are interwoven, and instructors should keep both in mind when teaching *Night*. For both go into a process of returning a trace of life to the corpse that stares into the eyes of Eliezer—and of the reader—at the end of the memoir.

Jewish Teachings Provide Path to Recovery

In Wiesel's memoir the recovery of value and meaning in life is tied to the recovery of Jewish teaching; the process of recovery is dialectically tied to the tale of this devastating loss. "There comes a time," Wiesel has said, "when only those who do believe in God will cry out to him in wrath and anguish". His memoir is just such an outcry.

The process of recovering what was lost begins with his brief account of what was lost, as Wiesel describes his life as a Hasidic adolescent who studied Talmud during the day and at night would "weep over the destruction of the Temple". In Wiesel's account of his passage from his Hasidic world into the Nazi antiworld, we see various dimensions of the Nazi assault on the sacred tradition that defined Eliezer's soul. In keeping with the Nazi practice of planning actions according to the Jewish holy calendar, we see that on the seventh day of Passover, a day of special observance and miraculous significance, the Germans arrested the Jewish leaders in Sighet; that they chose the Sabbath for the day of the Jews' expulsion; and that they made the period just following Rosh Hashanah into an occasion for mass selections. God had designated certain days when holiness would enter time, and the Nazis chose those days to erase the holy from time.

Just as the holiness of Jewish time comes under assault, the holiness of Jewish prayer unravels. When their transport arrives at Auschwitz [concentration camp], Eliezer and the others find themselves saying the Kaddish, the prayer for the dead, for themselves. "I don't know whether," says Eliezer, "during the history of the Jewish people, men have ever before recited Kaddish for themselves". His rebellion against God manifests itself in a play on a Jewish prayer, when at Rosh Hashanah he wonders,

> How could I say to Him: Blessed be Thou, Almighty Master of the Universe, who chose us among all nations to be tortured day and night, to watch as our fathers, our mothers, our brothers end up in the furnaces?

And yet the prayer, which is itself a trace of the divine presence, has a life of its own. For when Eliezer sees that Rabbi Eliahu's son has abandoned his father, he remembers, "in spite of myself, a prayer formed inside me, a prayer to this God in whom I no longer believed". It was a prayer that he should never abandon his own father, as Rabbi Eliahu's son had done.

To be sure, the memoir *Night* is itself a kind of prayer that Wiesel should never abandon his father—both the father he remembers in the memoir and the Father in whom he could no longer believe. For just as he remembers the Nazis' murder of his father, so does he remember the Nazis' murder of God. Indeed, the murder of God is a pivotal scene in the memoir: it happens when a child is hanged before the prisoners assembled at Buna [concentration camp]. "For God's sake, where is God?" Eliezer hears a man behind him ask. "And from within me, I heard a voice answer: 'Where He is? This is where—hanging here from this gallows . . .'". This memory of the murder of God harbors a testimony to what is at stake in the act of remembrance. The Talmud teaches that creation itself is sustained by the breath of children. And, according to a Jewish tradition, only the prayers from our children reach God's ear, for their lips are untainted by sin. When children are silenced God grows deaf. Words lose their meaning, and human beings lose their humanity.

What is at stake in this memory of the murder of God, then, is the idea of a human being and the dearness of a human life. "At Auschwitz, not only man died, but also the idea of man," Elie Wiesel has said. That idea dies with the death of a Jewish teaching and tradition concerning the holiness of every human being. The loss of that sense of holiness underlies humanity's illness of indifference from which Wiesel seeks a recovery.

Indifference Is an Illness of the Soul

Like the memory of the loss of the divine presence, the memory of human indifference harbors both an indictment and a testimony. And, just as the memory of God's death is part of an effort to recover even a negative relation to God, the memory of this indifference is an attempt to reawaken the divine image in the human being. For that image lives precisely in the care and concern offered to other human beings, which is precisely what the Nazis set out to destroy. Indeed, the title of the Yiddish edition of *Night* conveys just such a testimony: *Un di velt hot geshvign* ("And the World Remained Silent").

Wiesel underscores this illness when he and his father enter Auschwitz, smell the odor of burning flesh, and see babies thrown alive into pits of flames. Eliezer says that he could not believe that humanity would tolerate such a horror, to which his father replies, "The world? The world is not interested in us. Today, everything is possible, even the crematoria . . .". The

Elie Wiesel in New York City, 1986. Wiesel was awarded the Nobel Prize in 1986, and, soon after, he and his wife, Marion, established the Elie Wiesel Foundation for Humanity, an organization rooted in the memory of the Holocaust that works to combat indifference, intolerance, and injustice.

Nazis relied on the world's indifference toward the torture and murder of the Jews. And, once they had the Jews locked into the concentrationary universe, they cultivated that indifference among the Jews themselves. This indifference was a key part of the assault on the soul.

Following selection after Rosh Hashanah, those marked for the gas chambers "were standing apart, abandoned by the whole world". And when Eliezer tries to help his father, the head of a block tells him, "In this place, there is no such thing as father, brother, friend. Each of us lives and dies alone". In this place designed to murder Jews, a Jew is not a Jew. For with this collapse of all human relation comes the complete collapse of the human being as a someone.

This imposed illness from which the survivor seeks recovery overwhelms Eliezer most profoundly on the death of his father. If the tale of his own death turns on a single moment, this is that moment. "His last word had been my name," he confesses. "He had called out to me and I had not answered". It was as though he no longer knew his name or had a name. What began with having his name erased by the number A-7713 ended in this silence, into which was gathered a silencing of the human image and the divine spark that animates the human being. Three pages later the corpse is staring back at the survivor, with eyes that have never left him. But this "never" is tied to another dimension of the recovery at work in the memoir. . . .

Recovery Through Testimony

When teaching *Night* in the contexts of Holocaust memoirs, one should keep several points in mind. First are the various expressions of a defining feature of the Holocaust, namely the assault not only on human beings but on the notion of a human being. The Nazis understand the value of a human being to lie in an accident of nature, that is, in "race." Further, the Nazi sees in himself absolutely no connection to any other "race," so that he has no obligation to anyone. The Jew, on the other hand, represents the teaching that every human being is created in the image of the infinite one and that each of us stands in a divinely commanded, ethical relation to other human beings. When one teaches *Night* the Jew must not be forgotten.

Second, there is the multilayered issue of recovery and the effort to return to life through an act of testimony. Some survivors try to recover a sense of humanity; others try to recover a relation to the divinity. All struggle to recover a sense of meaning and value. And all are moved by a sense of urgency that would stir the world from the sleep of indifference. That we have these testimonies demonstrates the abiding trace of something infinitely precious, despite the Nazi attempt to annihilate it. The one who could not find a listener now asks us to listen. Therefore we become part of the Jew's project to return to life: we are transformed into messengers. This transformation too is an open-ended aspect of the survivor's recovery and return to life: those who receive the message transmitted in *Night* and other memoirs can receive it only by transmitting it in turn.

Finally, students who gaze into the mirror at the end of *Night* should be reminded that the aim of this study is not to succumb to despair or to be left in such a state. They must struggle to move, as Wiesel himself moved, from *Night* to *Dawn* to *Day* (the titles of his first three books). They must find a way to rejoice and give thanks—not for the evil of the Holocaust, certainly, but for the fact that it was evil. Which means there is something good and holy at stake in this study. For in this study something infinitely precious is placed in our care. Therefore we must answer the questions that the first murderer failed to answer: Where is your brother? And what have you done?

Social Issues
in Literature

CHAPTER 3

Contemporary
Perspectives on Genocide

Turkish Government Still Denies World War I–Era Armenian Genocide

Gail Russell Chaddock

Gail Russell Chaddock is a staff writer for the Christian Science Monitor.

In the following viewpoint, the author argues that the term "genocide" has been used only relatively recently, but the concept has been around for centuries. The author contends that distinguishing what is or is not considered genocide is difficult to distinguish, and because of this, genocide isn't easily recognized by all parties or nations involved, the Turkish government among them. The author also asserts that this denial, however, may be detrimental to the public discussion of genocide or other acts of human suffering during times of war.

The 20th century may have coined the term "genocide," but it did not invent the notion that one group improves its lot by annihilating another.

Euphemisms of Genocide

When 13th-century Mongol horsemen swept across Asia to the gates of Vienna, they made it a policy to kill every man, woman, and child in any city that resisted their advance. Contemporary accounts tallied the dead in the millions.

For a less brutal account, take a close look at the north-wing pediment of the US Capitol. The sculpted figure in the lower right corner is a dejected Indian chief, flanked by his family and a grave. Artist Thomas Crawford described this

Gail Russell Chaddock, "Reflections on the Unthinkable," *Christian Science Monitor*, April 27, 2000. Reproduced by permission from Christian Science Monitor, (www. csmonitor.com).

corner of his work: the "extinction" of the American Indian; the pediment, which was completed in 1863, is called: "Progress of Civilization."

Over the last millennium, humanity has grappled with ways to curb this harshest face of war, especially to make some distinction between fighters and noncombatants. From the 10th into the 12th centuries, Christian church councils debated the terms of a "just war." Soldiers developed their own approach to this issue: Codes of medieval chivalry extended protection to noncombatants. Professional militaries in the 18th century turned this distinction into codes of conduct. And by the end of the 20th century, international conventions formally defined—and outlawed—the practice of genocide altogether.

Nonetheless, the last century began and ended with some of the most brutal assaults on civilians in human history. These include the expulsion of Ottoman Armenians from their ancient homeland in World War I, the systematic annihilation of European Jews and other groups in World War II and slaughter of hundreds of thousands in Rwanda in 1994, and the revival of the concept of "ethnic cleansing" in such places as Cambodia (1975), and more recently, Bosnia, Kosovo, Sudan, and East Timor.

Recognizing Genocide

For those on the receiving end of genocide or "ethnic cleansing," recognition of what was done often comes late, if at all. World news media have been slow to pick up on what was actually happening in a genocide, especially one that occurs in the context of a war. After the fact, the victors or those with the best-organized lobby may weigh in more heavily in sorting out suffering than others caught up in a tragedy. The battle over who did what to whom, when, and how often goes on in scholarly and diplomatic circles decades after the events.

The Holocaust was barely mentioned in the years immediately after World War II. It was not until the 1960s that accounts of survivors were widely disseminated. And Armenian survivors of the 1915 death march are still lobbying strenuously for recognition of their ordeal as a "genocide."

Denial Is Destructive

In response to such concerns, many European nations, along with Canada and Australia, passed legislation outlawing writing or speech that denies the Holocaust. This month, British historian David Irving lost a $3 million libel suit against an American writer who labeled him as a Holocaust denier. (Irving has written that Jews were not killed in gas chambers and that Nazi dictator Adolf Hitler did not order the annihilation of European Jewry.)

"It's a very destructive thing when people deny the Holocaust. Banning that discussion prevents some destructive and hurtful public discussions," says Steve Hochstadt, professor of history at Bates College in Lewiston, Maine.

The term used to describe such events is important, because a key aspect of genocide is denial that it is occurring or has occurred, experts say. Nazi officials developed language for the Holocaust that disguised its purpose, such as "special handling" for execution or "final solution" for mass extermination. Groups of victims forced into early mobile gas chambers (vans that redirected the exhaust into the cargo area) were referred to in official documents as "the load."

"Early writing about what was going on in Germany referred to anti-Semitism, pogroms, atrocities. But none of these terms really described what was going on," says Raoul Hilberg, retired professor of political science at the University of Vermont and author of a landmark book on the Holocaust, "The Destruction of the European Jews" (1961).

At the same time, there are dangers with putting the Holocaust in an "academic ghetto" and "not realizing in the process that what happened in World War II was a broad-scale attack on humanity. Poles and Russians were also victims of the whole anti-human activity of Nazi Germany and its allies," he adds.

The Armenian Battle for Recognition

Armenians have carried their battle for recognition of "genocide" into national and state legislatures. In the United States, some 20 states have passed resolutions calling for recognition of an Armenian "genocide." (President Clinton and the US State Department use terms such as "tragedy" to describe these events.) In 1987, the European Parliament adopted a resolution that said that Turkey could not be accepted into the European Union until they ended their denial of the genocide—a position recently reaffirmed by the Rome City Council.

"The Turkish government as part of its efforts to deny and cover up the genocide has consistently tried to use evasive and euphemistic terminology to avoid using the term 'genocide.' They are trying to downgrade it to a civil conflict or domestic unrest," says Aram Hamparian, executive director of the Washington-based Armenian National Committee. "It's an extremely dangerous message to send if what is sent is that genocide can be committed and forgotten," he adds.

Turkish activists and officials insist that the Armenian expulsions were a desperate wartime measure—not part of a genocide plan—and that Armenians outside the Russian war front were not attacked.

"Even during the years of the relocation, and the confrontation, you see Armenians living peacefully in Istanbul and in government posts, ambassadors serving in European capitals. You didn't find that in Nazi Germany," says Guler Koknar, executive director of the Assembly of Turkish American Associations.

Distinguishing Genocide from Other Forms of Suffering

The distinction between a "genocide" and other forms of human suffering and brutality is not always clear. The term genocide refers to "an organized attempt to annihilate a group of people," and it "inherently has a structure," says Dr. Hilberg. "For example, Albanians [in Kosovo] were not wiped out the way Armenians in southeast and eastern Turkey were in the Ottoman Empire," he says.

"In Bosnia, well before the numbers of people killed reach figures even close to comparable to the Holocaust, everyone was aware of it. The news media had published it thoroughly and people were worried about stopping it. Whereas in the 1940s, when a million Jews had already been killed, there was hardly a ripple in the news media," Hilberg says.

The United Nations and Other Organizations Must Address Ethiopian Genocide

Farah A. Farah

Farah A. Farah is the director of the Centre for Development Research and Advocacy, a research and development organization based in London, England. Ogaden Online provides coverage of political and economic issues relative to Ogaden and the Horn of Africa.

In the following article Farah A. Farah expresses frustration that the international community has been silent on the issue of genocide in the Ogaden region of Ethiopia. Crimes against humanity are common in Ethiopia, but the massacre of civilians has been exceptionally brutal in Ogaden. National Security Forces and high-ranking government officials are supervising the slaughter and deprivation, according to Farah. Victims and survivors are demanding that the perpetrators be arrested and prosecuted. Farah suggests that the international community has a moral duty to uphold the Convention on the Prevention of the Crime of Genocide. Farah also states that the United States could invoke its Genocide Accountability Act, which allows arrest and prosecution of perpetrators of genocide living within the nation's borders.

In April 2006, a horrible mass murder got momentum and reached new heights in the Ogaden region of Ethiopia. Over the course of five months, more than 2200 civilians were slaughtered and estimated 120,000 individuals were driven out of the country by the Ethiopian National Defence forces (ENDF). A campaign of terror was undertaken against de-

Farah A. Farah, "Ethiopian Genocide Victims Deserve Justice," Ogaden Online, January 12, 2008. Reproduced by permission.

fenceless civilians. Women and underage girls were gang raped. Torture, mass killing, detention and disappearance were and are still common. Villages were burnt down, resulting in hundreds of thousands to be forcefully displaced. To make matters worse, dislodged communities (with their livestock) were denied access to drinking water.

Though the inhuman and degrading treatment inflicted on the communities was (and still remains to be) widespread all over the region, its degree varied from zone to zone. Wardher, Korahay, Degahbur and Fik zones were the epicentre of the campaign. In every standard, what happened in Dagahbur and Fik during this period amounts to genocide. Surely many renowned International Human Rights groups described it as a genocide.

Where Is the International Outcry?

The depressing question that many victims and survivors ask themselves is why the international communities are silent on the issue. It is painful and indeed disappointing that they do not know why they deserve to be treated so inhumanely. It is equally disappointing that no one has an answer when or where these atrocities will end. The very security forces funded and trained by the US (as part of war on terror) have been terrorising these vulnerable and defenceless society with impunity. Surely [Ethiopian prime minister] Meles [Zenawi] and his associates have misused the wider objectives of the war on terror badly. They diverted it terribly to dealing with their domestic critics and constantly tried to embroil US in regional crisis.

Ogaden Region Atrocities Rampant

Nowhere is this abuse more acute than Ogaden Region where the regime is brutal and unkind enough to burn and/or bury the people alive. Will they get justice or will Meles and his

Peter Omot is a member of the Ethiopian ethnic minority of Anuak who lives in Minnesota. He holds Omot Obang Olom, governor of Ethiopia's Gambella region, responsible for the massacre of four hundred of his ethnic kin in an attack in 2003. AP Images.

cronies get away with the crimes? Will the criminals be held accountable for the killings, tortures, detentions etc they have committed?

Violent Crimes Commonly Occur in Ethiopia

Crimes against humanity are common and institutionalised in Ethiopia. It was late 2003 when Gambellas were massacred by the National Security Forces. Former Deputy Minister of Federal Affairs, Dr. Gabreab Baranbaras was coordinating the process. However Abbay Tsahay [Abay Tsehaye](former Minister of Federal Affairs) now security adviser of the Prime Minister and General Samora Yunus (Chief Staff of Armed Forces) were the main protagonists closely supervising and giving the necessary directions. Before, Gambellas, it was Oromos who suffered the wrath of the Government and its consequences. No action was taken against those directly responsible for the crimes. This shows that Meles Zenawi was (and still is) guilty of complicity at best. Dr. Gabreab was transferred to Tigrai Region and he now heads Regional Health Bureau.

In Ogaden, the picture is even darker. Still [Abay Tsehaye] and General Samora are directly involved in the massacre. They unrepentantly continue the process though now greater in scale. Particularly Mr. [Abay] does constantly fly to Jijiga to evaluate the impact, reward those who have inflicted more damages and punish who haven't done enough. Sadly, he personally chaired the meeting in which the regional cabinet approved collective punishment. Similarly, General Samora has visited Dagahbur recently and urged the army to do more [to] crack down [on] the dirty pastoralists (as he put it). Following his return from Dagahbur, the army has immediately started to intensify the killings and other damages they were undertaking.

Other perpetrators include:

- Tawlde Berhe: EPRDF [Ethiopian People's Revolutionary Democratic Front] representative and the de facto regional administrator
- Brg. General Quarter: Commander of Eastern Division
- Colonel Wandituru: Commander of 32nd Brigade
- Da'uud Mahamed: Head of ruling Party
- Abdi Omar: Head of Regional Security Sector

More than 200 others working in the security apparatus and the regional government are known to have participated in this terror and massacre campaign.

Estimates of the genocide vary from thousands to tens of thousands. However, regardless of the exact figure, what is clear is that the architects of this infamous genocide have so far eluded justice.

Not only has the Government killed, tortured, detained, displaced or gang raped. It has also starved the whole population, denying them any access to food and drinking water.

Ethiopian Regime Still Supported by West

Therefore, the victims, survivors and those who lost their beloved ones are now demanding the arrest and prosecution of those who committed these horrendous crimes. They would like to see Zenawi and others held accountable for what they did [to] the innocent civilians. Truly the current Ethiopian regime led by Zenawi has been committing uglier crimes than [former Yugoslavian president Slobodan] Milosevic and [former Liberian president] Charles Tailor. But the regime still enjoys considerable support from Western countries. This is really unacceptable to powerless victims.

Until now the Gambella genocide architects have not been prosecuted in any court of justice, within or outside Ethiopia, because of other priorities by the US and western countries.

This has encouraged practicing another slaughter in conflict torn Ogaden once again, where government army forces are accused by human rights organisations of mass murder and starvation policy that claimed nearly
million innocent lives.

Years of massacre campaign and rampages has been accompanied by starvation policy, the recent UN [United Nations] mission in the region gave premonitions that the situation in the region has all [the] hallmarks of Darfur [a region in Sudan in conflict where human rights groups claim genocide is taking place] in [the] making.

John Holmes, UN Under-Secretary for Humanitarian affairs, briefed the Security Council after visiting the region that the food and goods blockade will be lifted immediately but it is still in place.

He urged incumbent Prime Minister Zenawi to allow independent UN mission to investigate atrocities committed. As the starvation deaths increase, Meles is trying to subvert and obstruct independent UN mission.

International Community Has Moral Duty

Majority of international community are party to the Convention on the Prevention of the Crime of Genocide, and as such, all governments have signed both to prevent and to punish acts of genocide, therefore they have moral duty to uphold their commitment and bring justice [to] all senior military and regional officials identified.

A detailed report published by advocacy organisations described the situation as Genocide and called for international intervention.

The recent report by Centre for Development Research Advocacy (CDRA) investigated whether the atrocities qualified as Genocide, an examination team sent to Ogaden and neighbouring countries to meet the survivors concluded that the answer is yes. This is an important report, because it expands the usage of the term "Genocide" to include tribally targeted mass killings, rapes and a large number of population displacement perpetrated in the course of military crackdown.

What has emerged from this report anyway, is the grand design to torture, starve, brutalise an entire Ogaden population and ultimately murder a quarter of them had been going on since April.

Since Zenawi's minority TPLF [Tigrayan People's Liberation Front] regime came to power with barrel of gun nearly two decades ago, state repression and denial of basic rights for 80 million Ethiopians became rampant and widely institutionalised.

In his bid to hang onto power for a fifth term and ensure his own survival in the face of international condemnation and embarrassment from last 2005 elections, the regime resorted to snuffing more people.

The army officers who masterminded the Gambella killings were simply following the orders as the Nazis did before them and will continue to do so in Ogaden unless those in charge are tried for crimes against humanity.

The United States Could Invoke Genocide Accountability Act

The international community, particularly, the United States government, with its powerful Genocide Accountability Act, could be invoked here to stop more killings in Ogaden. This piece of legislation together with ICC [International Criminal Court] rules would permit all perpetrators of genocide living in US to be prosecuted within the US legal system, regardless of their citizenship or the location of their crimes.

Like the US, this is the only way the international community can prevent further killings and deny safe havens for genocidaires and ensure they are brought to justice.

In the previous decades we saw genocide occur in other parts of the world. Today we confront the reality of ongoing genocide in Ogaden and it's shameful if we don't stop now and talk about [this] a century later in a manner analogous to Armenian genocide.

The international community, particularly the US, and citizens everywhere must take a stand today to prevent and to stop acts of genocide.

It is incumbent on every nation in the world to ensure that such crimes against humanity are not tolerated. The not so distant tragedy in Rwanda should act as a wake up call.

Pro-Sudan Advertising Should Not Be Accepted While Genocide Continues

Philip Chaffee

Philip Chaffee was a student at the Columbia University Journalism School when this article was published.

While the front pages of the New York Times *carried negative information about Sudan and the plight of the citizens of Darfur, the newspaper accepted an insert from Sudan's government extolling the virtues of its economy, states Philip Chaffee in the following article. The paper reaped nearly $1 million in ad revenue from the insert. Human rights activists protested the newslike insert, saying it was propaganda for a genocidal regime. The* Times *defended its decision to publish the ad, stating that doing so was consistent with the paper's belief in the free flow of ideas, even if the* Times *did not endorse Sudan's politics. The communications firm that produced the insert has also published ad inserts for Rwanda and the Democratic Republic of Congo.*

On Monday, March 20, [2006,] the *New York Times* included a full-color advertising insert with a picture of the Nile at sunset and a large caption reading, "Sudan: The Peace dividend—Prosperity could lie ahead after years of conflict".

What followed was eight pages of newspaper-like stories that extolled the Sudanese economy. Most of the stories included interviews with high government officials. "Ministers are frustrated that coverage of Sudan in the international media has focused almost exclusively on the fighting between

Philip Chaffee, "How The Times Sells Genocide: A Paid Insert Touts the Sudan as Massacres Continue," *New York Press*, April 12, 2006. Reproduced by permission of the author.

rebels and Arab militias in the western province of Darfur," read the lead article. "Beyond the headlines, there is genuine optimism about the prospects for Sudan's future."

But this advertisement appeared at the very moment that the United States government was reaffirming that genocide was indeed taking place in Sudan's western province of Darfur—and that *New York Times* reporters and columnists were continuing their relentless reporting and criticism of what many are calling a holocaust.

After the advertisement was published, human rights activists began to question the insert and its publication. What exactly was the Sudanese government trying to accomplish with such seemingly blatant propaganda? What is Summit Communications, the company that had produced not just this insert, but several others advertising other countries in the weeks prior? And why had the *Times* decided to publish an advertisement for Sudan, after the front pages of the newspaper had included so much negative information about a nation that had descended into anarchy?

"I think this was a terrible moral mistake," said Eric Reeves, a Smith College professor who has waged a personal campaign to stop the genocide in Darfur. "Would they"—referring to the editors of the *Times*—"have accepted ads from Germany in the wake of Kristallnacht? Obviously not. There is some threshold in which a newspaper must make decisions."

Times Defends Insert

According to Allan Siegal, the standards editor at the *Times*, there was some debate over the publication of the insert, though he didn't take part in it. Beyond the meeting, Siegal said that there were very specific policies regulating "advertorials" such as the Sudan insert. Regulations include an "Advertising Supplement" disclaimer on every page and a different typeface for the articles, Siegal wrote in an e-mail.

Siegal was also quick to explain that "news and ads occupy opposite sides of a church-state wall. Newsroom editors don't approve or disapprove advertising, just as ad sales people don't pass upon the news content."

Steph Jesperson, who attended the meeting over the Sudan insert as the director of advertising acceptability for the *Times*, declined to comment, referring questions to a *Times* spokeswoman. The spokeswoman, Catherine J. Mathis, wrote in an e-mail, "The *Times* has vigorously reported on the Sudan and our editorials have condemned the actions the Sudanese government has taken against its citizens. We accepted this special advertising section, however, in our strong belief that all pages of the paper—news, editorial and advertising—must remain open to the free flow of ideas. In accepting it, we do not endorse the politics, trade practices or actions of the country or the character of its leaders."

John Prendergast, a Sudan activist for the International Crisis Group (ICG), responded angrily, "It's one thing to allow for different views to be aired. But to take money for an ad for three pages lined up against an occasional article or op-ed seems like a capitulation to commercial needs."

Times Reaps About $1 Million

The *Times* did take a significant amount of money for the ad. The *New York Daily News* reported that the insert cost $929,000, but Mathis denied this figure. In 2003, however, Summit Communications, the advertising agency involved, struggled with the government of Madagascar to receive a $105,000 fee for a similar insert. Prices have risen considerably since then, so it seems safe to say that hundreds of thousands are involved.

This "represents blood money," wrote Nicholas Kristof in a statement released last week, after many readers and reporters asked for the *Times* columnist's reaction to the Sudan story.

"It tarnishes a newspaper I love." But Kristof refuted the argument that publishing the insert made the *Times* complicit in genocide.

"If this supplement were a racist tract saying that all Zaghawa tribe members are scum and should die," wrote Kristof, "that would be so offensive that I would agree that it should be blocked. On the other hand, this advertising isn't racist; this is just pabulum."

What Motivated Sudan?

So why would Sudan spend over a million dollars to publish such pabulum? The average reader, knowing the situation in Darfur, would probably be put off by puff pieces that started with "Estimates of how much oil lies beneath Sudan's desert sands vary from 3 billion barrels to 10 billion," and then complain that "Chevron might well be interested in returning to Sudan, but there is a major obstacle: the U.S. government ban on investment in the country, introduced in 1997, still remains in force."

Eric Reeves, the anti-genocide activist, said that the Sudanese government believes in "incremental victories," and was probably not hoping for a huge shift in public opinion with the advertisement. "They know the vast majority of people will immediately see it's propaganda. If they persuade even a few people that the Sudan is being misrepresented, that it's a good investment opportunity, maybe that will result in the White House or Congress being lobbied."

United States Not About to Drop Sanctions

So far, such lobbying is almost unheard of, said Ted Dagne, a Sudan expert at the Congressional Research Service. "The recent house version of the Darfur Accountability Act adds more sanctions," said Dagne. "I have not heard from anybody other than the government of the Sudan that they would like the sanctions to be dropped."

Sudan has also mounted a considerable smear campaign against prominent activists on the Darfur issue, said both Reeves and John Prendergast. Reeves said that one Sudan front-group published a personal attack that was sent to every faculty member at his university, as well as many students and alumni.

"They're attempting to smear anyone who is opposed to them," said Prendergast.

The advertising insert is much more innocuous, compared to that campaign. At the center of the advertising controversy is Summit Communications, the firm that spent a year putting together the Sudan insert.

Summit Communications Has Assisted Other Nations

Summit Communications is a public-relations company based in New York (although registered as a corporation in Europe) that publishes advertorials through "an exclusive relationship with the *New York Times*" and promises prospective countries the "opportunity to provide greater input and review of our reports' content in conveying their message to the influential readership of the *New York Times*."

Summit Communications appears to approach its clients at the very height of government. Although it had published ad inserts for Rwanda and the Democratic Republic of Congo (DRC) in the week before the Sudan insert, the press agents at embassies for both countries had never heard of the inserts. Neither, for that matter, had the office of the ambassador at the Sudanese embassy.

"We are independent of any government agency direct or indirect," wrote Summit Communications in an unsigned e-mail, the only way they would agree to communicate. "Our selection of countries is based on more than 10 years of experience and our own international knowledge." Such knowledge has enabled Summit Communications to advertise for such countries as Libya, Saudi Arabia and Pakistan.

Summit Has Access to Highest Ranking Officials

The inserts themselves rely almost completely on interviews with high government officials. Summit Communications' Web site even includes video interviews with Sudan's vice president, Ali Mohammed Taha, as well as an interview with Joseph Kabila, the president of the DRC. That the embassies of three countries contacted about Summit Communications—Rwanda, Madagascar, and Sudan—knew nothing about the company suggests its relationships are at the very highest levels of African regimes.

Suffering Continues in Darfur

Vice President Taha, who appeared frequently in the advertising insert as well as in the online video interview, is reportedly under investigation by the International Criminal Court for connection to war crimes in Darfur. Meanwhile the situation in Darfur itself, said Eric Reeves, is only getting worse.

"We have now entered what may be the greatest season of death in Sudan for the last 20 years. Four hundred thousand-plus people have died in Darfur. That excludes the Nuba mountains, all other regions suffering at Khartoum's [the Sudan government's] hands," said Reeves.

"When things are worst, you say the most outlandish things to lure investors."

Mass Human Tragedy Numbs Individual Ability to Act

Paul Slovic

Paul Slovic is a professor of psychology at the University of Oregon.

Paul Slovic's research has led him to the conclusion that people are more able to respond with caring to a single individual in need than a mass of humanity. Genocide and crimes against humanity do not motivate individuals, who even seem indifferent, due to the psychological mechanisms that fail to spark an emotional response. In the following article, Slovic states that it is more difficult for people to feel human suffering on a massive scale. Psychophysical numbing—or compassion fatigue—numbs humans to react to situations that seem beyond their ability to affect change. Slovic recommends forcing rational, as well as emotional, thought to motivate people to take action.

"If I look at the mass I will never act. If I look at the one, I will." This statement, uttered by Mother Teresa captures a powerful and deeply unsettling insight into human nature: Most people are caring and will exert great effort to reserve "the one" whose needy plight comes to their attention. But these same people often become numbly indifferent to the plight of "the one" who is one of many in a much greater problem. This indifference has been evident during the past 4 ½ years in the Darfur region of Western Sudan, where more than 200,000 people have been murdered by government sponsored militias and at least 2.5 million more have been forced to flee their burned-out villages.

Unfortunately Darfur is not an isolated incidence of genocide. Others, such as the Holocaust in Nazi Germany, are well

Paul Slovic, "Psychic Numbing and Genocide," APA Online Psychological Science Agenda, November 2007. Reproduced by permission of the author.

known. In a deeply disturbing book [*A Problem from Hell: America and the Age of Genocide*] that won the Pulitzer Prize for Samantha Power, Darfur can be seen as but the latest of a long string of genocides dating back to 1915. Power notes that in every instance America and the rest of the world looked away.

Why don't these massive crimes against humanity spark us to action? Why do good people ignore mass murder and genocide? Unfortunately there are no simple answers to these questions. Every episode of mass murder is unique and raises unique social, economic, military, and political obstacles to intervention. But the repetitiveness of such atrocities, ignored by powerful people and nations, and by the general public, calls for explanations that may reflect some fundamental deficiency in our humanity—a deficiency that, once identified, might possibly be overcome.

Large Numbers Cannot Convey True Magnitude of Atrocities

One fundamental mechanism that may play a role in many, if not all, episodes of mass-murder neglect involves the capacity to experience affect, the positive and negative feelings that combine with reasoned analysis to guide our judgments, decisions, and actions. Research shows how the statistics of mass murder or genocide, no matter how large the numbers, fail to convey the true meaning of such atrocities. The numbers fail to spark emotion or feeling and thus fail to motivate action. Genocide in Darfur is real, but we do not "feel" that reality. I examine below ways that we might make genocide "feel real" and motivate appropriate interventions. Ultimately, however, I conclude that we cannot only depend on our intuitive feelings about these atrocities but, in addition, we must create and commit ourselves to institutional and political responses based upon reasoned analysis of our moral obligations to stop the mass annihilation of innocent people.

My search to develop a psychological explanation for apathy toward mass murder and genocide has led to a theoretical framework that describes the importance of emotions and feelings in guiding decision making and behavior. Perhaps the most basic form of feeling is affect, the sense (not necessarily conscious) that something is good or bad. Affect plays a central role in what have come to be known as "dual-process theories" of thinking. As [S.] Epstein has observed: "There is no dearth of evidence in every day life that people apprehend reality in two fundamentally different ways, one variously labeled intuitive, automatic, natural, non-verbal, narrative, and experiential, and the other analytical, deliberative, verbal, and rational".

Two Types of Thinking Influence Behavior Regarding Genocide

[K.E.] Stanovich and [R.F.] West labeled these two modes of thinking *System 1* and *System 2*. One of the characteristics of System 1, the experiential or intuitive system, is its affective basis. Although analysis (*System 2*) is certainly important in many decision-making circumstances, reliance on affect and emotion is generally a quicker, easier, and more efficient way to navigate in a complex, uncertain and sometimes dangerous world. Many theorists have given affect a direct and primary role in motivating behavior.

Underlying the role of affect in the experiential system is the importance of images, to which positive or negative feelings become attached. Images in this system include not only visual images, important as these may be, but words, sounds, smells, memories, and products of our imagination.

[D.] Kahneman notes that one of the functions of System 2 is to monitor the quality of the intuitive impressions formed by System 1. Kahneman and [S.] Frederick suggest that this monitoring is typically rather lax and allows many intuitive judgments to be expressed in behavior, including some that are erroneous. This point has important implications that will be discussed later. In addition to positive and negative affect, more nuanced feelings such as empathy, sympathy, compassion, and sadness have been found to be critical for motivating people to help others. As [C.D.] Batson put it, ". . . considerable research suggests that we are more likely to help someone in need when we 'feel for' that person . . ."

One last important psychological element in this story is attention. Just as feelings are necessary for motivating helping, attention is necessary for feelings. Research shows that attention magnifies emotional responses to stimuli that are already emotionally charged. Research I shall describe here demonstrates that imagery and feeling are lacking when large losses of life are represented simply as numbers or statistics. Other research shows that attention is greater for individuals and loses focus and intensity when targeted at groups of people. The foibles of imagery and attention impact feelings in a manner that can help explain apathy toward genocide.

Another important link to feelings comes from [J.] Haidt, who argues that moral intuitions (akin to System 1) precede moral judgments. . . .

Valuing Human Lives and Psychophysical Numbing

How *should* we value the saving of human lives? If we believe that every human life is of equal value (a view likely endorsed by System 2 thinking), the value of saving N lives is N times the value of saving one life. An argument can also be made for judging large losses of life to be disproportionately more serious because they threaten the social fabric and viability of a group or society, as in genocide.

How *do* we actually value humans' lives? Research provides evidence in support of two descriptive models linked to affect and System 1 thinking that reflect values for lifesaving profoundly different from the normative models just described. Both of these descriptive models are instructive with regard to apathy toward genocide.

The first of these, the psychophysical model, is based on evidence that an affective response and the resulting value we place on saving human lives may follow the same sort of "psychophysical function" that characterizes our diminished sensitivity to a wide range of perceptual and cognitive entities as their underlying magnitudes increase. Constant increases in the magnitude of a stimulus typically evoke smaller and smaller changes in response. Applying this principle to the valuing of human life suggests that a form of *psychophysical numbing* may result from our inability to appreciate losses of life as they become larger. The importance of saving one life is great when it is the first, or only, life saved, but diminishes marginally as the total number of lives saved increases. Thus, psychologically, the importance of saving one life is diminished against the background of a larger threat—we will likely not "feel" much different, nor value the difference, between saving 87 lives and saving 88, if these prospects are presented to us separately. [D.] Fetherstonhaugh, [P.] Slovic, [S.M.] Johnson, and [J.] Friedrich documented this potential for diminished sensitivity to the value of life—i.e., "psychophysical numbing"—in the context of evaluating people's willingness to fund various lifesaving interventions.

Although a psychophysical model can account for the disregard of incremental loss of life against a background of a large tragedy, it does not fully explain apathy toward genocide because it implies that the response to initial loss of life will be strong and maintained, though with too little change, as the losses increase. Evidence for a second descriptive model, better suited to explain apathy toward genocide, follows.

Psychological theories and data confirm what keen observers of human behavior have long known. Numerical representations of human lives do not necessarily convey the importance of those lives. All too often the numbers represent dry statistics, "human beings with the tears dried off," that lack feeling and fail to motivate action. How can we impart the feelings that are needed for rational action? Attempts to do this typically involve highlighting the images that lie beneath the numbers. For example, organizers of a rally designed to get Congress to do something about 38,000 deaths a year from handguns piled 38,000 pairs of shoes in a mound in front of the Capitol. Students at a middle school in Tennessee, struggling to comprehend the magnitude of the holocaust, collected 6 million paper clips as a centerpiece for a memorial.

A Victim with a Face and a Name Arouses More Compassion

When it comes to eliciting compassion, the identified individual victim, with a face and a name, has no peer. Psychological experiments demonstrate this clearly, but we all know it as well from personal experience and media coverage of heroic efforts to save individual lives. The world watched tensely as rescuers worked for 2 ½ days [in October 1987] to rescue 18-month-old Jessica McClure, who had fallen 22 feet into a narrow abandoned well shaft. Charities such as Save the Children have long recognized that it is better to endow a donor with a single, named child to support than to ask for contributions to the bigger cause.

But the face need not even be human to motivate powerful intervention. A dog stranded aboard a tanker adrift in the Pacific was the subject of one of the most costly animal rescue efforts. Columnist Nicholas Kristof, noted cynically that a single hawk, Pale Male, evicted from his nest in Manhattan, aroused more indignation than two million homeless Sudanese.

Vivid images of recent natural disasters in South Asia and the American Gulf Coast, and stories of individual victims there, brought to us through relentless, courageous, and intimate news coverage, certainly unleashed a tidal wave of compassion and humanitarian aid from all over the world. Perhaps there is hope that vivid, personalized media coverage of genocide could motivate intervention.

Perhaps. Research demonstrates that people are much more willing to aid identified individuals than unidentified or statistical victims. But a cautionary note comes from a study by [D.A.] Small, [G.] Loewenstein, and [Paul] Slovic, who gave people leaving a psychological experiment the opportunity to contribute up to $5 of their earnings to Save the Children. In one condition respondents were asked to donate money to feed an identified victim, a seven-year-old African girl named Rokia. They contributed more than twice the amount given by a second group asked to donate to the same organization working to save millions of Africans from hunger. A third group was asked to donate to Rokia, but was also shown the larger statistical problem (millions in need) shown to the second group. Unfortunately, coupling the statistical realities with Rokia's story significantly *reduced* the contributions to Rokia. . . .

Writer Annie Dillard reads in her newspaper the headline "Head Spinning Numbers Cause Mind to Go Slack." She struggles to think straight about the great losses that the world ignores: "More than two million children die a year from diarrhea and eight hundred thousand from measles. Do we blink? [Soviet dictator Joseph] Stalin starved seven million Ukrainians in one year, [Cambodian leader] Pol Pot killed two million Cambodians. . ." She writes of "compassion fatigue" and asks, "At what number do other individuals blur for me?". . .

Overcoming Obstacles

Clearly there are serious political obstacles posing challenges to those who would consider intervention in genocide, and physical risks as well. What I have tried to describe here are the psychological obstacles centered around the difficulties in wrapping our minds around genocide and forming the emotional connections to its victims that are necessary to motivate us to overcome these other obstacles.

Are we destined to stand numbly and do nothing as genocide rages on for another century? Can we overcome the psychological obstacles to action? There are no simple solutions. One possibility is to infuse System 1 with powerful affective imagery such as that associated with Hurricane Katrina and the South Asian tsunami. This would require pressure on the media to do its job and report the slaughter of thousands of innocent people aggressively and vividly, as though it were real news. Another way to engage our experiential system would be to bring people from Darfur into our communities and our homes to tell their stories.

As powerful as System 1 is when infused with vivid experiential stimulation (witness the moral outrage triggered by the photos of abuse at the Abu Ghraib prison in Iraq), it has a darker side. We cannot rely on it. It depends upon attention and feelings that may be difficult to arouse and sustain over time for large numbers of victims, not to speak of numbers as small as two. Left to its own devices, System 1 will likely favor individual victims and sensational stories that are closer to home and easier to imagine. Our sizable capacity to care for others may also be overridden by more pressing personal interests. Compassion for others has been characterized by Batson, [K.] O'Quin, [J.] Fultz, [M.] Vanderplas, and [A.] Isen as "a fragile flower, easily crushed by self-concern". Faced with genocide, we cannot rely on our moral intuitions alone to guide us to act properly.

A more promising path might be to force System 2 to play a stronger role, not just to provide us with reasons why genocide is wrong—these reasons are obvious and System 1 will appropriately sense their moral messages. As Kahneman argues, one of the important functions of System 2 is to monitor the quality of mental operations and overt behaviors produced by System 1.

This monitoring function is particularly critical. The psychological account presented here indicates that we cannot depend solely upon our *moral intuitions* to motivate us to take proper actions against genocide. We thus need to invoke our capacity for deliberate, rational thought, i.e. *moral argument*, to guide us. Such moral deliberation led to the drafting, in 1948, of the Genocide Convention, designed to prevent such crimes against humanity from ever happening again. Yet this convention has proven ineffective in numerous episodes of genocide that have occurred after World War II. It is time to examine this failure in light of the psychological deficiencies described here and design legal and institutional mechanisms that will compel us to respond properly when signs of genocide come to our attention.

I particularly hope that those with expertise in international law, human rights, and politics will heed the lessons from psychology as they address the challenge of curtailing mass murder and genocide in the 21st Century.

For Further Discussion

1. In his Nobel Prize acceptance speech (Chapter 1), Elie Wiesel states that the world community must be vigilant about addressing future attempts at genocide and be prepared for counterattacks. Yet it seems that acts of genocide, such as those occurring in Ethiopia described by Farah A. Farah (Chapter 3), still continue. To what extent should other nations become involved in preventing or ending acts of genocide? Is it the duty of the United States, as a leading world power, to set the agenda and take the lead in combating genocide wherever it occurs?

2. Simone Gigliotti (Chapter 2) promotes the concept that the Nazis' system for moving the Jews from their homes and transporting them in degrading conditions caused a breakdown in societal norms. Identify a present-day situation that has caused societal breakdown.

3. As described by Jack Kolbert (Chapter 2), Wiesel used silence as a tool to indicate that words could not capture the horrific life in the concentration camps. How did the silences affect your reading or understanding of Wiesel's environment? What did the silences mean to you? Identify three other art forms or events that use silence to create impact.

4. In Chapter 3, Gail Russell Chaddock describes how Turkey's political influence has motivated the U.S. government to overlook claims of World War I–era genocide of Armenians. Given Turkey's strategic geographic position and importance to U.S. security, do you think it is, or is not, acceptable for the U.S. government to refuse to condemn the Armenian genocide? What information and beliefs helped you reach your decision?

5. David L. Vanderwerken (Chapter 2) promotes the viewpoint that Wiesel's experiences in the concentration camps were the opposite of the kinds of experiences a young person needs to grow, build character, and take his or her place in the world. However, in David Patterson's viewpoint (Chapter 2), Wiesel has overcome his hardships and recovered a sense of value and meaning in life. Can you reconcile these apparently contradictory viewpoints? How do you think Wiesel used his experiences to become the man he is today?

For Further Reading

Anne Frank, *Anne Frank: The Diary of a Young Girl.* New York: Doubleday, 1995.

John Hersey, *The Wall.* New York: Knopf, 1950.

Imre Kertész, *Fateless.* Evanston, IL: Northwestern University Press, 1992.

Lawrence L. Langer, *Art from the Ashes: A Holocaust Anthology.* New York: Oxford University Press, 1995.

Primo Levi, *Survival in Auschwitz: The Nazi Assault on Humanity.* New York: Simon & Schuster, 1996.

Dalia Ofer and Lenore J. Weitzman, eds., *Women in the Holocaust.* New Haven, CT: Yale University Press, 1998.

Irene Gut Opdyke, *In My Hands: Memories of a Holocaust Rescuer.* New York: Anchor Books, 2001.

Art Spiegelman, *Maus: A Survivor's Tale,* New York: Pantheon Books, 1991.

Elie Wiesel, *The Accident.* New York: Hill and Wang, 1962.

———, *Dawn.* New York: Hill and Wang, 1961.

———, *The Gates of the Forest.* New York: Holt, Rinehart & Winston, 1966.

———, *The Town Beyond the Wall.* New York: Holt, Rinehart & Winston, 1964.

Bibliography

Books

Michael Barnett   *Eyewitness to a Genocide: The United
                    Nations and Rwanda.* Ithaca, NY:
                    Cornell University Press, 2003.

Robert McAfee   *Elie Wiesel: Messenger to All
Brown   Humanity.* Notre Dame, IN:
                   University of Notre Dame Press,
                   1983.

Jacqueline A.   *The Laughter of the Oppressed: Ethical
Bussie   and Theological Resistance in Wiesel,
                   Morrison, and Endo.* New York:
                   Continuum, 2007.

Colin Davis   *Elie Wiesel's Secretive Texts.*
                   Gainesville: University Press of
                   Florida, 1994.

Terrence Des Pres *The Survivor: An Anatomy of Life in
                   the Death Camps.* New York: Oxford
                   University Press, 1976.

Ted L. Estess   *Elie Wiesel.* New York: F. Ungar, 1980.

Saul Friedländer   *Nazi Germany and the Jews.* 2 vols.
                   New York: HarperCollins, 1997–2007.

Daniel Jonah   *Hitler's Willing Executioners: Ordinary
Goldhagen   Germans and the Holocaust.* New
                   York: Knopf, 1996.

Rosemary
Horowitz and
Miriam Klein
Kassneoff, eds.

Elie Wiesel and the Art of Storytelling.
Jefferson, NC: McFarland, 2006.

Robert Jay Lifton

*The Nazi Doctors: Medical Killing and
the Psychology of Genocide.* New York:
Basic Books, 1986.

Deborah E.
Lipstadt

*Denying the Holocaust: The Growing
Assault on Truth and Memory.* New
York: Free Press, 1993.

Linda Melvern

*Conspiracy to Murder: The Rwandan
Genocide.* New York: Verso, 2006.

Donald E. Miller
and Lorna
Touryan Miller

*Survivors: An Oral History of the
Armenian Genocide.* Berkeley:
University of California Press, 1999.

Hazel Rochman
and Darlene Z.
McCampbell

*Bearing Witness: Stories of the
Holocaust.* New York: Orchard, 1995.

Alvin H.
Rosenfeld and
Irving Greenberg,
eds.

*Confronting the Holocaust: The
Impact of Elie Wiesel.* Bloomington:
Indiana University Press, 1978.

John K. Roth

*A Consuming Fire: Encounters with
Elie Wiesel and the Holocaust.* Atlanta,
GA: John Knox Press, 1979.

Simon P.
Sibelman

Silence in the Novels of Elie Wiesel.
New York: St. Martin's Press, 1995.

David S. Wyman   *The Abandonment of the Jews:*
America and the Holocaust,
1941–1945. New York: Pantheon,
1984.

Periodicals

Mark Chmiel   "The Political Varieties of Sacred
Remembrance: Elie Wiesel and U.S.
Foreign Policy," *Journal of Church
and State,* vol. 40, no. 4, Autumn
1998.

Mildred L. Culp   "Wiesel's Memoir and God Outside
Auschwitz," *Explorations in Ethnic
Studies,* January 1981.

Charlayne   "A Crisis Up Close," *Essence,* March
Hunter-Gault   2008.

Jack Kolbert   "Elie Wiesel: The Holocaust Survivor
as Chronicler," *West Virginia
University Philological Papers,* vol. 44,
1998–1999.

Harold P. Maltz   "Holocaust Fiction and National
Historical Memory: Elie Wiesel, the
Fifth Son," *Theoria,* vol. 81/82,
October 1993.

D.G. Myers   "Responsible for Every Single Pain:
Holocaust Literature and the Ethics
of Interpretation," *Comparative
Literature,* vol. 51, no. 4, Autumn
1999.

Zsuzsanna
Ozsvath and
Martha Satz

"The Audacity of Expressing the
Inexpressible: The Relation Between
Moral and Aesthetic Considerations
in Holocaust Literature," *Judaism: A
Quarterly Journal of Jewish Life and
Thought*, Spring 1985.

Karl A. Plank

"The Survivors Return: Reflections
on Memory and Place," *Judaism: A
Quarterly Journal of Jewish Life and
Thought*, Summer 1989.

Susan Rubin
Suleiman

"Problems of Memory and Factuality
in Recent Holocaust Memoirs:
Wilkomirski/Wiesel," *Poetics Today*,
vol. 21, no. 3, Fall 2000.

Index